jQuery Tools UI Library

Learn jQuery Tools with clear, practical examples and get inspiration for developing your own ideas with the library

Alex Libby

BIRMINGHAM - MUMBAI

jQuery Tools UI Library

First published: February 2012

Production Reference: 1160212

Published by Packt Publishing Ltd.
Livery Place
35 Livery Street
Birmingham B3 2PB, UK.

ISBN 978-1-84951-780-5

www.packtpub.com

Cover Image by Mudimo Okondo (mudimo@okhabitat.com)

Credits

Author
Alex Libby

Reviewers
Jake Kronika

Deepak Vohra

Mudimo Okondo

Acquisition Editor
Kartikey Pandey

Technical Editors
Vanjeet D'souza

Pramila Balan

Project Coordinator
Joel Goveya

Proofreader
Kevin McGowan

Indexer
Tejal Daruwale

Production Coordinator
Aparna Bhagat

Cover Work
Aparna Bhagat

About the Author

Alex Libby holds a Masters' degree in e-commerce from Coventry University, and currently works as a Sharepoint Technical Analyst for a well-known parts distributor based in the UK. Alex has used jQuery Tools as part of his daily work for the last 18 months, and enjoys the challenge of working out simple solutions to common issues using jQuery and jQuery Tools, particularly using a progressive enhancement methodology.

Prior to this, he spent a number of years in IT Support, working in the banking, health, and defense publishing industries. Alex has also been instrumental in releasing the current version of jQuery Tools as featured in *jQuery Tools UI Library*, and enjoys helping out others in the forums to figure out solutions to their issues when using the software.

I would like to thank my family and friends for their support while writing the book. I would also like to thank Tero Piiranen for releasing such an awesome library, and to Brad Robertson and Mudimo Okondo for helping with tips, bug fixes for the current release of jQuery Tools, the awesome flower pictures used in the demos, and inspiration for the book.

I would particularly like to thank Joy Jones, without whom I probably would never have considered writing—you've done more than you probably could ever realize, Joy!

About the Reviewers

Jake Kronika, a web designer and developer with over 15 years of experience, brings to this book a strong background in front-end development with JavaScript and jQuery, as well as significant training in server-side languages and frameworks.

Having earned a Bachelors of Science degree in Computer Science from Illinois Wesleyan University in 2005, with a minor in Business Administration, Jake went on to become Senior User Interface (UI) Specialist for Imaginary Landscape LLC, a small web development firm in the Ravenswood neighborhood on the north side of Chicago. In this role, the foundations of his strengths in Cascading Style Sheets (CSS) and JavaScript (JS) were honed and finely tuned.

From there, Jake went on to work for the Sun-Times News Group, owner of the Chicago Sun-Times and numerous suburban newspapers in Chicago. It was in this role that he was initially exposed and rapidly gained expert skills with the jQuery framework for JS.

Following intermediate positions as Technology Consultant with Objective Arts, Inc, and as UI Prototyper for JP Morgan Chase, Jake moved across the United States to Seattle, WA, where he assumed his current role of Senior UI Software Engineer with the Cobalt Group, an online marketing division of Automatic Data Processing Inc (ADP) Dealer Services. Since 1999, he has also operated Gridline Design & Development (so named in 2009), a sole proprietorship for web design, development, and administration.

Jake has reviewed two other books by Packt Publishing, namely, *Django JavaScript Integration: AJAX and jQuery*, authored by Jonathan Howard (2011) and *JQuery UI 1.8: The User Interface Library for jQuery*, authored by Dan Wellman (2011).

Deepak Vohra is a consultant and a principal member of the NuBean.com software company. Deepak is a Sun Certified Java Programmer and Web Component Developer. He has worked in the fields of XML and Java programming and J2EE for over five years.

Deepak is the co-author of *Pro XML Development with Java Technology* published by Apress and was the technical reviewer for *WebLogic: The Definitive Guide* published by O'Reilly. Deepak was also the technical reviewer for the Course Technology PTR book *Ruby Programming for the Absolute Beginner*, and the technical editor for the Manning Publications book *Prototype and Scriptaculous in Action*.

Deepak is also the author of the Packt Publishing books *JDBC 4.0 and Oracle JDeveloper for J2EE Development, Processing XML Documents with Oracle JDeveloper 11g*, and *EJB 3.0 Database Persistence with Oracle Fusion Middleware 11g*.

www.PacktPub.com

Support files, eBooks, discount offers and more

You might want to visit www.PacktPub.com for support files and downloads related to your book.

Did you know that Packt offers eBook versions of every book published, with PDF and ePub files available? You can upgrade to the eBook version at www.PacktPub.com and as a print book customer, you are entitled to a discount on the eBook copy. Get in touch with us at service@packtpub.com for more details.

At www.PacktPub.com, you can also read a collection of free technical articles, sign up for a range of free newsletters and receive exclusive discounts and offers on Packt books and eBooks.

http://PacktLib.PacktPub.com

Do you need instant solutions to your IT questions? PacktLib is Packt's online digital book library. Here, you can access, read and search across Packt's entire library of books.

Why Subscribe?

- Fully searchable across every book published by Packt
- Copy and paste, print and bookmark content
- On demand and accessible via web browser

Free Access for Packt account holders

If you have an account with Packt at www.PacktPub.com, you can use this to access PacktLib today and view nine entirely free books. Simply use your login credentials for immediate access.

Table of Contents

Preface

"Let's face it—do you really need drag and drop, resizable windows, or sortable lists on your website...?"

If the answer is no, then welcome to "jQuery Tools UI Library"!

jQuery Tools is a compact, powerful library that contains enough components to provide the most important functionality on any website. Many UI libraries contain a myriad of components, such as list boxes, ranges, sortable lists, and the like. While this can be used to build a range of online-based applications that are useful in company intranets, for example, it is not so useful when building normal websites.

Websites are built to present information and to look good—jQuery Tools is designed to enhance any site that uses them, while harnessing the power that modern JavaScript techniques can offer. With jQuery Tools, you are not tied to any predefined HTML, CSS structures, or strict programming rules—you can include the library in your pages and start to use its functionality immediately. The tools are designed to be customized to your liking, while maintaining the core functionality that goes to make up JQuery Tools.

If you're a newcomer to jQuery Tools, and want to explore the functionality available, this is the book for you. With easy to follow step-by-step instructions, you'll find what you need to get you going with using this library, and discover how you can implement some complex functionality, with just a few lines of code.

So let's get on with it...

What this book covers

Chapter 1, Getting Started with jQuery Tools UI Library, introduces you as the reader to the library billed as the "missing UI library for the Web". It explains how to get hold of jQuery Tools, outlines the tools you will need to develop webpages which use this functionality, and outlines some of the best practices to use with jQuery Tools.

Chapter 2, Getting Along with your UI Tools, delves into each part of the jQuery Tools UI library, and how to implement the basic tools into your website. Within each part of the UI library, a walk-through demonstration is included, as well as a more advanced example of what can be achieved using the library.

Chapter 3, Form Tools, introduces the form functionality within jQuery Tools. It outlines how to submit and validate content in a form, as well as entering numbers using RangeInput and dates using DateInput. It also demonstrates how to ensure all content is validated correctly, using HTML5 standards.

Chapter 4, jQuery Tools Toolbox, introduces a small collection of tools which, in most cases, can either be used on their own, or as part of one of the main tools from the Library. It notes that although some of the technologies are becoming outdated (thanks to the modern advances of HTML, CSS3 and JavaScript), they can still perform some useful functions within your projects.

Using jQuery Tools in WordPress is an additional PDF available for download from Packt's website, which accompanies this book. It contains some useful ideas and examples for using jQuery Tools within the confines of a content management system. Although the examples are based around the well-known and popular WordPress™ system, the principles could easily be applied to other, similar systems.

Who this book is for

This book is great for those new to the jQuery Tools library. It is assumed that you won't have any prior knowledge of the library, but will likely have a basic knowledge of JavaScript syntax and concepts. This book will allow you grasp the basics of using the library, and how to use it to build striking, customisable webpages.

Conventions

In this book, you will find a number of styles of text that distinguish between different kinds of information. Here are some examples of these styles, and an explanation of their meaning.

Code words in text are shown as follows: "We will now build a custom effect called `myEffect`, which we will add to the overlay code."

A block of code is set as follows:

```
<!-- first overlay. id attribute matches our selector -->
<div class="simple_overlay" id="mies1">
  <!-- large image -->
    <img src="photos/barcelona-pavilion-large.jpg" />
  <!-- image details -->
  <div class="details">
    <h3>The Barcelona Pavilion</h3>
    <h4>Barcelona, Spain</h4>
    <p>The content ...</p>
  </div>
</div>
```

When we wish to draw your attention to a particular part of a code block, the relevant lines or items are set in bold:

```
<!-- first overlay. id attribute matches our selector -->
<div class="simple_overlay" id="mies1">
  <!-- large image -->
    <img src="photos/barcelona-pavilion-large.jpg" />
  <!-- image details -->
  <div class="details">
    <h3>The Barcelona Pavilion</h3>
    <h4>Barcelona, Spain</h4>
    <p>The content ...</p>
  </div>
</div>
```

New terms and **important words** are shown in bold. Words that you see on the screen, in menus or dialog boxes for example, appear in the text like this: "Clicking the **Next** button moves you to the next screen."

 Warnings or important notes appear in a box like this.

 Tips and tricks appear like this.

Reader feedback

Feedback from our readers is always welcome. Let us know what you think about this book—what you liked or may have disliked. Reader feedback is important for us to develop titles that you really get the most out of.

To send us general feedback, simply send an e-mail to feedback@packtpub.com, and mention the book title through the subject of your message.

If there is a topic that you have expertise in and you are interested in either writing or contributing to a book, see our author guide on www.packtpub.com/authors.

Customer support

Now that you are the proud owner of a Packt book, we have a number of things to help you to get the most from your purchase.

Downloading the example code

You can download the example code files for all Packt books you have purchased from your account at http://www.packtpub.com. If you purchased this book elsewhere, you can visit http://www.packtpub.com/support and register to have the files e-mailed directly to you.

Errata

Although we have taken every care to ensure the accuracy of our content, mistakes do happen. If you find a mistake in one of our books—maybe a mistake in the text or the code—we would be grateful if you would report this to us. By doing so, you can save other readers from frustration and help us improve subsequent versions of this book. If you find any errata, please report them by visiting http://www.packtpub.com/support, selecting your book, clicking on the **errata submission form** link, and entering the details of your errata. Once your errata are verified, your submission will be accepted and the errata will be uploaded to our website, or added to any list of existing errata, under the Errata section of that title.

Piracy

Piracy of copyright material on the Internet is an ongoing problem across all media. At Packt, we take the protection of our copyright and licenses very seriously. If you come across any illegal copies of our works, in any form, on the Internet, please provide us with the location address or website name immediately so that we can pursue a remedy.

Please contact us at copyright@packtpub.com with a link to the suspected pirated material.

We appreciate your help in protecting our authors, and our ability to bring you valuable content.

Questions

You can contact us at questions@packtpub.com if you are having a problem with any aspect of the book, and we will do our best to address it.

1
Getting Started

If you've built web pages, or developed websites using HTML over the last few years, you will most likely have heard of jQuery—you may not have heard of jQuery Tools.

Web professionals all over the world have been trying to make the Internet a more usable place to visit, using JavaScript to try to overcome some of the shortcomings of HTML and CSS. jQuery's power and flexibility lie in its deceptive simplicity, making navigating a document, selecting elements on a page, and handling events, straightforward, while smoothing out any browser differences. There are a number of UI libraries available on the Internet that offer functionality based on jQuery. jQuery Tools is one of them—while although many libraries were designed to offer a wide variety of functionality, jQuery Tools was designed to offer only the functionality that is most useful on a normal website, in other words not a JavaScript application based site. Its small size belies its power and flexibility, offering a huge amount of functionality in just 4 KB.

In this chapter we shall learn:

- A little of the history of jQuery Tools, and some of its guiding principles
- How to download and install the library, or use the CDN links
- Some best practices for writing events and using the API

So let's begin...

jQuery Tools basics and rules: a primer

"Let's face it — do you really need drag-and-drop, resizable windows, or sortable lists in your web applications…?"

If the answer is no, then welcome to jQuery Tools! jQuery Tools were designed to provide a number of Web 2.0 goodies found on websites around the Internet, that can be extended, customized, and styled the way you desire. The principle aim of the tools is to provide a bare bones framework of functionality, that offers just the functionality needed, and nothing else — the API framework can then be used to extend the tools in a myriad of ways. With this in mind, let's take a look at the ethos of jQuery Tools in a little more detail.

The role of HTML

The jQuery Tools library was designed with a high degree of flexibility, where you can progressively enhance the functionality of a normal website, while still allowing for browsers that don't support JavaScript. When using the toolset, you are not limited to any particular HTML structure; you are free to use any suitable elements such as ul, ol, div, or dl at will. It is crucial to understand what you are doing, and how to choose the right element for your specific requirement. A root element, such as a div can equally be used, although this is not obligatory. For example, you could have an overlay's root element that contains a mix of HTML, images, forms, and Flash objects, as your overlaid information.

The role of JavaScript and jQuery

Although the JQuery Tools library was built using jQuery, it is, with the exception of FlashEmbed, not a prerequisite to using the Tools. While you can use the tools without any prior knowledge of jQuery, it can help with extending or enhancing the functionality within the library, and on your site. If you would like to delve more into using jQuery with the tools, then a useful place to start is by looking at selectors and object literals, such as in the following example:

```
// two jQuery selectors and a configuration given as an object literal
$("#content ul.tabs").tabs("div.panes > div", {
    // configuration variables
    current: 'current',
    effect: 'fade'
});
```

The preceding code can be split into two parts—the first part selects all `ul` elements with the class name of `tabs`, contained in a `div` called `content`, in a similar manner to CSS. The `tabs` functionality is then set to operate on all div elements held directly within the `div` with a CSS style class of `panes`. You can use a similar format of syntax when configuring any of the tools, although it would be wise to take care over typing the right number of brackets! Irrespective of which tool you use, you will need to encompass any script within a `$(document).ready()` block, so that the script can be loaded at the appropriate time—you may find it preferable to load the script into the footer of your website (this is required for some of the tools).

The role of CSS

jQuery Tools was designed to allow website designers to abstract code away from the main "block", and into separate style sheets. You will notice that CSS style names have been used where possible. This makes styling the code more flexible, as styles can be changed at will, without needing to change the main code—though it is not a recommended practice to mix CSS styles within JavaScript or HTML code. As an example, you can style an instance of an active tab within `tabs`:

```
$("ul.tabs").tabs("div.panes > div", {current: 'active'});
```

After that you can style the current tab with CSS as follows:

```
ul.tabs .active {
    color: '#fff';
    fontWeight: bold;
    background-position: 0 -40px;
}
```

This allows you to control the appearance of an instance of `tabs` completely, even down to changing the default style names used. This is useful if you already have existing styles which would otherwise conflict, or if you need to follow a particular CSS naming convention.

 The jQuery Tools website hosts a number of demos, which contain CSS style files that are available for you to use—it is worth checking these out to get a feel for the basics on styling the Tools. All of the demos are fully documented and use good CSS styling practices.

Using tools for graphic design and presentation

As a developer using jQuery Tools, you have a high degree of freedom when it comes to styling the Tools on your site. This means you can use pure CSS, images, or a mix of both within your designs.

CSS-based design

Using pure CSS within your design means a reduced reliance on images, as most (if not all) of the styles can be handled by using pure CSS. This is particularly true with the advent of CSS3, which can handle styles such as gradients in backgrounds, that would otherwise require images. However, it does mean that while pages are lightweight and easy to maintain, it is not possible to achieve everything using just CSS, at least up to version 2. The advent of CSS3 is beginning to change this, although your latest stunning design may not work in older browsers!

Image-based design

If images are more to your style, then the best method is to use an image sprite, which is the favored method within jQuery Tools. Sprites can be positioned exactly, using CSS, and as long as an appropriate image format is used, will display in most (if not all) browsers. This allows you to achieve exactly the look and feel you are after, without any compromise, although it will make pages heavier, and it could mean more use of scrollbars, if you have a large amount of content within a Tool (such as an Overlay).

CSS and image-based design

This method gives you the best of everything — CSS can be used to keep the page download times low, while images can be used where CSS styles are inappropriate in your environment. jQuery Tools uses both within its demos, you are equally free to use both within your own designs, with no restriction on CSS coding or the requirement to use frameworks.

Using tools for development

For the purposes of completing the exercises in this book, you will need a text editor. Most PCs will come with one — usually Notepad on Microsoft Windows, or TextEdit on Mac OS X. There are literally thousands available for free or low cost, with varying degrees of features.

If you are an existing developer, you will likely have your editor of choice already; for those of you who are new to editing, it is a matter of trying a few, and seeing which you prefer. There are some features I would recommend you enable or use:

- **View line numbers**: This feature is handy during validating and debugging any scripts that you write. This can be of particular help when requesting assistance in the forums, as others can indicate any line(s) at fault, and help provide a fix or workaround.

- **View syntax colors**: Most editors will have this feature switched on by default. This feature displays code using different colors, which helps you to identify different syntax, or broken mark-up or CSS rules.

- **Text wrapping**: This allows the editor to wrap code lines around onto the next line, which reduces the need to scroll through long lines of code when editing. It makes it easier to scroll through a nice, correctly indented, block of code.

You may also want an editor which allows you to upload files using FTP, or view your local directories. This avoids the need to go hunting for files in your OS's file explorer, or using an external FTP application to get copies of files, and cuts down the time it takes to edit files. To view the results of the experiments and samples, you will need a browser—jQuery Tools uses CSS3 styling, so a modern browser will provide the most feature-rich and design-rich experience. This includes the following:

- Firefox 2.0+
- Internet Explorer 7+
- Safari 3+
- Opera 9+
- Chrome 1+

Any of these browsers can be downloaded for free from the Internet. If you are using Internet Explorer or Firefox and if you do not already have them installed, it is strongly recommended that you also install or activate the appropriate developer toolbar for your chosen browser:

- **IE Developer Toolbar**: It is available from `http://www.microsoft.com/download/en/details.aspx?id=18359`

- **Firebug**: Developer tool for Firefox, which can be downloaded from `http://www.getfirebug.com`

- **Chrome**: This is already built in, and can be activated by right-clicking an element and selecting **Inspect element**

- **Safari**: You can activate its developer toolbar under the **Advanced** tab in Safari **Preferences**
- **Opera**: You can download its developer toolbar from `http://www.opera.com/dragonfly/`

All will be very useful in helping you debug your scripts, when designing sites that use jQuery Tools.

Downloading the library

The first thing we need to do is to get a copy of the jQuery Tools library, from the official website (`http://www.flowplayer.org/tools`).

The modular nature of jQuery Tools means that you can choose the components you want to download, or you can choose to download a copy of the entire library. This is important if you want to keep your pages as light as possible.

There are several options available for the purpose of downloading the jQuery Tools library: you can use the free CDN links (even for production use), download a custom version, or download an uncompressed version from the Github area.

If you include this statement in your code:

```
<script src=
  "http://cdn.jquerytools.org/1.2.6/jquery.tools.min.js">
</script>
```

You will have the following tools available:

- jQuery 1.6.4
- Tabs
- Tooltip
- Scrollable
- Overlay

The tools will be loaded with maximum performance no matter where your user is located on the globe. If you already have jQuery included on your page, you can simply remove it and use only the script `src` statement (as it already includes jQuery), or, if you prefer, insert the tools without jQuery link, for example:

```
<script src=
  "http://cdn.jquerytools.org/1.2.6/all/jquery.tools.min.js">
</script>
```

Then reference jQuery separately; the best practice is to use Google's CDN link, which is (at time of writing):

```
<script src=
  "http://ajax.googleapis.com/ajax/libs/jquery/1.6.4/jquery.min.js>
</script>
```

But I want more… using the CDN links

If you prefer, you can use one of the other CDN links provided for referencing jQuery Tools – CDN stands for **Content Delivery Network**, which is a high-speed network that allows fast provision of content around the world.

There are several advantages to using this method:

- If you've already been to a site where jQuery Tools have been used, then it will already be cached, and this means you don't have to download it again.
- Content is made available through local servers around the world, which reduces the download time, as you will get a copy of the code from the nearest server.

The following are some of the links available for you to use, more are available on the jQuery Tools website:

```
<!-- UI Tools: Tabs, Tooltip, Scrollable and Overlay -->
<script src=
  "http://cdn.jquerytools.org/1.2.6/tiny/jquery.tools.min.js">
</script>

<!-- ALL jQuery Tools. No jQuery library -->
<script src=
  "http://cdn.jquerytools.org/1.2.6/all/jquery.tools.min.js">
</script>

<!-- jQuery Library + ALL jQuery Tools -->
<script src=
  "http://cdn.jquerytools.org/1.2.6/full/jquery.tools.min.js">
</script>
```

For the purpose of this book, you should use the main CDN link, so that we can make sure we're all on the same page.

Rolling your own tools – using the download builder

The modular design of jQuery Tools allows you to pick and choose which components you need for your projects. If your project doesn't need all of the components, then it's good practice to only download those that you need, to reduce the page weight and keep page response time as low as possible.

The download builder (`http://flowplayer.org/tools/download/index.html`) produces minified versions of the tools you choose, into one file—this can include jQuery if desired. The default download (shown overleaf) includes the major tools, which are **Overlay**, **Tabs**, **Scrollable**, and **Tooltips**—you can change these selections to only download those components you need for a specific project. You can also choose to include jQuery 1.6.4 at the same time, which helps to cut down page load times, as explained earlier in this chapter.

Using Firebug

If you are using a debugger such as Firebug, you can test which tools are included and what are their versions by running the following command from the console:

```
console.dir($.tools);
```

You'll see something similar to the following screenshot:

```
>>> console.dir($.tools);
  ⊞ dateinput          Object { conf={...}, localize=function() }
  ⊞ expose             Object { conf={...} }
  ⊞ flashembed         Object { conf={...} }
  ⊞ history            Object { init=function() }
  ⊞ overlay            Object { conf={...}, addEffect=function() }
  ⊞ rangeinput         Object { conf={...} }
  ⊞ scrollable         Object { conf={...}, autoscroll={...}, navigator={...} }
  ⊞ tabs               Object { conf={...}, slideshow={...}, addEffect=function() }
  ⊞ tooltip            Object { conf={...}, dynamic={...}, addEffect=function() }
  ⊞ validator          Object { conf={...}, messages={...}, localize=function(), more... }
    version            "1.2.5"
```

You can see each tool you have included and the version number. If you drill down a little deeper into these global settings you will see each tool's default configuration values (a good source for documentation!), which are discussed more extensively in the important *Using Global Configuration* section of this chapter.

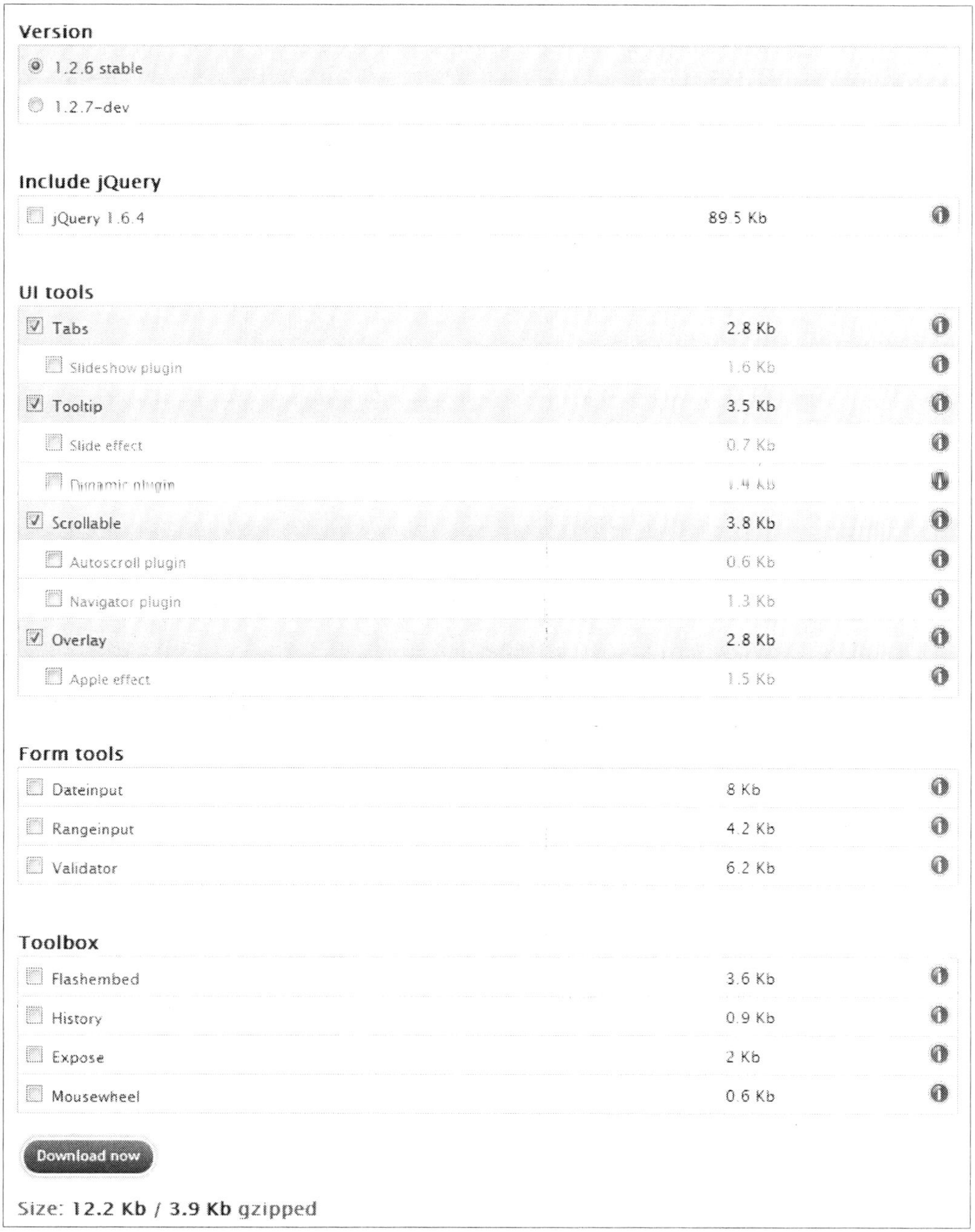

Version

- ◉ 1.2.6 stable
- ◯ 1.2.7-dev

Include jQuery

☐ jQuery 1.6.4	89.5 Kb	ⓘ

UI tools

☑ Tabs	2.8 Kb	ⓘ
☐ Slideshow plugin	1.6 Kb	ⓘ
☑ Tooltip	3.5 Kb	ⓘ
☐ Slide effect	0.7 Kb	ⓘ
☐ Dynamic plugin	1.4 Kb	ⓘ
☑ Scrollable	3.8 Kb	ⓘ
☐ Autoscroll plugin	0.6 Kb	ⓘ
☐ Navigator plugin	1.3 Kb	ⓘ
☑ Overlay	2.8 Kb	ⓘ
☐ Apple effect	1.5 Kb	ⓘ

Form tools

☐ Dateinput	8 Kb	ⓘ
☐ Rangeinput	4.2 Kb	ⓘ
☐ Validator	6.2 Kb	ⓘ

Toolbox

☐ Flashembed	3.6 Kb	ⓘ
☐ History	0.9 Kb	ⓘ
☐ Expose	2 Kb	ⓘ
☐ Mousewheel	0.6 Kb	ⓘ

Download now

Size: **12.2 Kb** / **3.9 Kb** gzipped

Including and initializing the tools

The next step is to include the Tools on your page—you can either use one of the CDN links as shown earlier, or include a custom version using the download builder.

Then you need to initialize the tools—they all follow the same pattern, which starts with a jQuery selector, followed by the initialization function (or constructor), and its configuration object. Here is an example using the scrollable tool, where elements are contained within an element whose ID is `scroll`:

```
$("#gallery").overlay({
    fixed: true,
    closeOnClick: false
})
```

When using the API format, the constructor will always return the jQuery object that is a collection of the elements that are selected by the selector, which you can then continue to work with, as shown in the following code snippet:

```
// return elements specified in the selector as a jQuery object
    var elements = $("div.scrollable").scrollable();

elements.someOtherPlugin().Click(function() {
    // do something when this element is clicked
});
```

Using global configurations

Sometimes you may find that you want to specify a default configuration value, so that you can avoid the need to set the same settings repeatedly in your code. jQuery Tools has a global configuration option, `$.tools.[TOOL_NAME].conf`, which is:

```
// all overlays use the "apple" effect by default
$.tools.overlay.conf.effect = "apple";
```

This means you then don't need to include it in your JavaScript code for Overlay:

```
// "apple" effect is now our default effect
$("a[rel]").overlay();
```

You can then override it if you need to:

```
$("a[rel]").overlay({effect: 'default'});
```

If you want to change multiple configuration options at a global level, you can use the jQuery built-in `$.extend` method:

```
$.extend($.tools.overlay.conf, {
    speed: 400,
    effect: 'apple'
});
```

 The list of various configuration settings can be found on each individual tool's documentation page.

You can use something like Firebug to get more details of the global configuration, by typing in this command `console.dir($.tools.overlay.conf);` which will produce images similar to this:

```
>>> console.dir($.tools.overlay.conf);
    close                       null
    closeOnClick                true
    closeOnEsc                  true
    closeSpeed                  "fast"
    effect                      "default"
    fadeInSpeed                 "fast"
    fixed                       true
    left                        "center"
    load                        false
    mask                        null
    oneInstance                 true
    speed                       "normal"
 +  start                       Object { top=null, left=null }
    target                      null
    top                         "10%"
    zIndex                      9999
```

Best practices for events and API calls

In this section we will look at some of the best practices for each of the tools, including how to use the API, write events, and design plug-ins using jQuery Tools functionality.

Application Programming Interface (API)

As time goes by, you will want to extend your skills with jQuery Tools—you can do this by using its API, which was built to expose methods and access properties for each tool in the library. The API hides the internal values from the outside world, which is good programming practice.

To begin with, you need to create an instance of the API for that tool, such as:

```
//get access to the API
Var api = $("#scroller").data("scrollable")
```

You will notice that the argument passed to `data` in brackets is that of the tool name—this could be changed to `overlay`, for example. When you have the API instance created, you can start using it, by calling its methods:

```
//do something upon scroll
    api.onSeek(function() {
        // inside callbacks the "this" variable is a reference
        // to the API
        console.info("current position is: " + this.getIndex())
    });
```

You can easily see the available API methods a jQuery Tool is using with Firebug, which can act as a good source of information:

```
>>> console.dir($("#nav ul").data("tabs"));
click                              function()
destroy                            function()
getConf                            function()
getCurrentPane                     function()
getCurrentTab                      function()
getIndex                           function()
getPanes                           function()
getTabs                            function()
next                               function()
onBeforeClick                      function()
onClick                            function()
prev                               function()
```

Using the API means that you are less likely to need all of jQuery's DOM methods, as most of the methods you need will be available from within the tool. This includes methods to retrieve information, as well as set values or invoke actions.

You can even chain methods onto an API instance of a tool, as the method will always return the API:

```
// normal API coding that programmers are accustomed to
var index = $("#example").data("tabs").click(1).getIndex();
```

If your selector returns multiple instances and you want to access a particular API, you can do following:

```
// select the correct instance with a jQuery selector
var api = $(".scrollable:eq(2)").data("scrollable");

//or with traversing methods. it is just a matter of taste
api = $(".scrollable").eq(2).data("scrollable");
```

jQuery Tools events

Within the API, each tool can respond to events as specific points in time where an action needs to be completed. A good example of this is **Scrollable** — each time you scroll through images, for example, you could fire the onSeek event. You could add your own custom responses (or listeners) each time this happens — this is particularly useful if you want to extend the default behavior of the tools.

 Event listeners are often referred to as **callbacks** — both terms are equally valid.

Before and after events

You can add your own custom functionality to any of the Tools, as they provide the before and after event methods for this purpose. These actions can equally be cancelled using the onBefore event, such as in this example, which uses the onBeforeClick callback for tabs:

```
$("#example").tabs(".panes > div", {

    // here is a "normal" configuration variable
    current: 'active',

    // here is a callback function that is called before the
    // tab is clicked
     onBeforeClick: function(event, tabIndex) {

    // the "this" variable is a pointer to the API. You can do
    // a lot with it.
    var tabPanes = this.getPanes();
```

```
    /*
    By returning false here the default behavior is cancelled.
    This time another tab cannot be clicked when "terms" are not
    accepted
    */
    return $(":checkbox[name=terms]").is(":checked");$(
        ":checkbox[name=terms]").is(":checked");
    }

});
```

Supplying events

There are three different ways of supplying event listeners in the tools:

Within the configuration

The first, and easiest, option is to include event listeners as part of your code directly:

```
$(".tabs").tabs({
    // do your own stuff here
    onClick: function() {
        ...
        var tabPanes = this.getPanes();
    }
});
```

A downside of using this option means that you can't specify multiple instances of the same callback in the code. For example, including two different `onClick` methods in the same configuration would result in an error.

 In the previous example, the `this` variable is a reference to the Tabs API.

Using jQuery's bind method

The second method follows that used within jQuery, where you can assign multiple listeners consecutively, in a chain:

```
// first callback
$(".tabs").bind("onClick", function() {
    // "this" is a reference to the DOM element
    var ulElement = this;
    ...
    // another one
}).bind("onClick", function() {
    // another one
    ...
});
```

Using this method offers greater flexibility, as it allows you to remove specific event listeners within the code, or to bind several instances of the same event listener within the same call. In the preceding example, the CSS .tabs selector is set to perform two actions when the onClick event is triggered by any of the tabs using that selector. The tools also allow you to bind the same event listener to multiple event trigger types in a single call:

```
// the same event listener is called before and after
// a tab is clicked
$(".tabs").bind("onBeforeClick onClick", function() {
});
```

It is strongly recommended that you try to familiarize yourself with this functionality in some depth, if you aren't already familiar with event binding — there is plenty of good reference material available in this area.

Supplying listeners from the API

The tools also allow you to supply one or more callbacks from within the API:

```
// grab the API with jQuery's data method
var api = $(".tabs").data("tabs");

// supply an event listener
api.onBeforeClick(function()  {
    // supply another
}).onClick(function() {
    ...
});
```

You can use the internal this variable as a reference to any of the Tools APIs, which will allow you to chain multiple event listeners together; this is more suitable for developers who are not already familiar with jQuery:

```
// loop through each instances
$(".tabs").each(function() {
    ...
    // assign the onClick listener to a single instance
    $(this).data("tabs").onClick(function() {
    ...
    });
});
```

The event object

If you are using callbacks, it is worth noting that the Tools adhere to the current W3C standards, when passing the `event` object as the first argument for each callback function:

```
// the event object is the first argument for *all* callbacks
// in jQuery Tools
api.onClick(function(event) {

   /* If you have multiple callbacks of the same type this prevents
      the rest of the callbacks from being executed. */
   event.stopImmediatePropagation();
   ...
   // retrieve the value returned by the previous callback function
   event.result;
   event.result;
   ...
   // whether CTRL, ALT, SHIFT, or ESC was being pressed
   var alt = event.altKey,
   ctrl = event.ctrlKey,
   shift = event.shiftMey,
   esc = event.metaKey;
   ...
   // this is how to get the original triggering element, such
   //  as a handle to the scrollable navigator item that was clicked
   // inside an onSeek event
   var element = e.originalTarget || e.srcElement;
});
```

Within the scope of jQuery Tools, the `preventDefault()` is identical to returning false from the callback; this is considered to be the accepted practice for cancelling the default event.

Creating jQuery Tools plugins

The Tools were designed to work in tandem with jQuery, which allows you to create jQuery Tools-based plugins. Using jQuery, you can easily alter or extend the default behavior of the tools, with the added benefit of being able to reference the Tools API, and use any number of callback functions. To give you some idea, here's a simple example of a plugin that uses Google Analytics to track each click, every time a tab is selected:

```
// create jQuery plugin called "analytics"
$.fn.analytics = function(tracker) {
```

```
    // loop through each tab and enable analytics
    return this.each(function() {

        // get handle to tabs API.
        var api = $(this).data("tabs");

        // setup onClick listener for tabs
        api.onClick(function(event, index)  {
            tracker.trackEvent("tabs", "foo", index);
        });

    });
};
```

 For those of you not familiar with writing jQuery plugins, you may like to look at the jQuery 1.4. *Plugin Development Beginner's Guide*, by Giulio Bai, published by Packt Publishing.

After you have included the plugin on your page, you can use the plugin in the following manner, which follows the standard format for developing the plugins:

```
// initialize tabs and the analytics plugin.
$("ul.tabs").tabs("div.panes > div").analytics(tracker);
```

jQuery Tools require that the tabs be initialized before the analytics plugin, so you cannot write:

```
$("ul.tabs").analytics(tracker).tabs("div.panes > div");
```

Using jQuery Tools plugins and effects

The design of jQuery Tools allows you to make full use of jQuery's chaining capabilities, which means you can create chain patterns, such as the following:

```
// initialize a few scrollables and add more features to them
$(".scroller").scrollable({circular: true}).navigator("#myNavi").
autoscroll({interval: 4000});
```

Here, the base Scrollable call will turn any element with the `.scroller` class into a scrollable and the Tools' minimalist design means you are free to then extend or alter the behavior by use of additional code or plugins, such as adding the navigator or autoscroll, whilst keeping code easier to read and file sizes smaller. The net result is that you can then set up a number of scrollables on a page, which are all activated using the same single line of code, but which contain their own local configuration values (this could equally be global). This decorator philosophy forms part of the whole ethos of jQuery Tools (and indeed jQuery as a whole). Most tools come with a number of plugins that are available for download, or you can add your own custom-built ones if desired.

Effects

Coupled with the plugin architecture available with most tools, you can also design your own effects for use with some of the tools. This will allow you to change the default behavior of the tool being used, whereas plugins would be used to extend that behavior. For example, you can add an effect to control how overlay opens or closes—an example of this is the apple effect, which comes with overlay:

```
// use the "apple" effect for the overlays
$("a[rel]").overlay({effect: 'apple'});
```

The use of additional effects means that you can hive off code into separate files, which makes the base overlay code smaller and more organized. You can then take this a step further by creating more effects that can be referenced from separate files, and dropped into your code as necessary. You could also set a specific effect to be used as your default effect, from within a global configuration; this reduces the need to specify in each instance it is used in your code. You can also achieve the same effect with configuration values—if you have a number of values that are set as part within an effect, you can then set these to apply by default at a global level, for every instance where this effect is used. For example, you may have an `explosionSpeed` value set in your effect—the following would turn it into a global configuration variable:

```
$.tools.overlay.conf.explosionSpeed = 500;
```

It is worth having a look at `http://gsgd.co.uk/sandbox/jquery/easing/`, the home of the jQuery Easing plugin; there are a number of effects there, that can be adapted for use within jQuery Tools.

Performance of jQuery Tools

A key design facet of jQuery Tools, as outlined by Yahoo's five rules of best practice, is that designers should try to reduce the number of images, stylesheets, and scripts that have to be downloaded. Yahoo argues that this is the key to improving the speed of your site, as most of the time spent looking at a site is from the front-end. The five rules created by Yahoo!, and to which jQuery Tools adheres, are:

1. Reduce the number of HTTP requests.
2. Use a CDN link, for incorporating scripts into your code where possible.
3. Add an `expires` header.
4. GZIP components where possible.
5. Minimize the JavaScript by compressing the code.

If you include the following script link in your code, you will be able to respect these five rules:

```
<script src="http://cdn.jquerytools.org/1.2.6/jquery.tools.min.js">
</script>
```

They can help to improve the performance of your site significantly and improve your website performance roughly by 70 to 80 percent! You are encouraged to use the CDN links that are made available, especially for production use; if you are concerned about the file size you should download a combined script that contains only those tools that you really need and follow the principles that are mentioned in this chapter.

Reduce the number of HTTP requests

A good practice is to minimize the number of separate JavaScript or CSS files used in a site—this helps to reduce the amount of time taken to fetch content from different sources. This is allowed for within jQuery Tools, which uses one combined JavaScript file when either downloading a custom build of the library, or using the CDN links.

jQuery Tools are available through CDN

There are a number of CDN links that are available for use—using these can result in a 15 to 20 percent increase in efficiency, in comparison to using manual, static links.

Adding an expires header

JQuery Tools are built with `expires` headers set on all of the tools, which makes them cacheable; this will reduce subsequent response times from each visit to a site by as much as 50 percent.

GZIP components

If gzipping has been enabled on a server, then this can help cut file sizes by as much as 65 percent; most modern browsers claim to be able to handle gzipping, when it has been enabled on a server. All jQuery Tools downloads available through the CDN links are gzipped, to help reduce download times.

Minifying JavaScript

jQuery Tools scripts are minified using Google Closure Compiler to reduce the file sizes and increase performance, as this yields a higher compression ratio than simply packing the same files.

Summary

In this chapter, we learned about:

- The basics of jQuery Tools, and some of the rules that it follows
- How to download a copy of the library or to use the CDN links provided
- Some of the best practices for writing events and API calls when using jQuery Tools

We discussed how you can leverage jQuery Tool's modular nature, to download only those components you need for your projects. We also looked at some of the rules and best practices that should be used when designing pages or projects that use jQuery Tools.

Now that we've learned about the basics of jQuery Tools, and how to install it, we're ready to start delving into using it, which is the subject of the next chapter.

2
Getting along with your UI Tools

"Actions speak louder than words…"

The sixteenth century writer, Michel de Montaigne, is often quoted with inventing this phrase, which the author believes is quite apt for jQuery Tools—after all, the best way to learn about new tools is to try to use them, right?

In the previous chapter, we learned a little about the whole ethos of jQuery Tools, and that the emphasis is placed less on the JavaScript code, but more on the ability of tools to be styled in lots of different ways, by changing the CSS and altering some of the configuration options of the tool being used.

It is time now to look at some of these tools in detail—this chapter (and the next) contains a number of projects which use various tools and showcase a bit of what can be achieved by using CSS and minimal JavaScript.

In this chapter we shall learn how to:

- Build a map lightbox effect using Google™ Maps
- Build a simple gallery, that showcases a number of images
- Construct a quicklink tooltip, to allow the purchase of a book
- Display images in a Polaroid-styled slideshow

So, as someone once said…"What are we waiting for..?" Let's get on with it...

 All of the images listed in this chapter's examples are available in the code download that accompanies this book.

UI tools – a template

Before we look at the examples in detail, let's set up the basic framework that will be used in each project. Open up your favorite text editor, and copy the following code:

```
<!DOCTYPE html>
<html>
  <head>
    <title>jQuery Tools standalone demo</title>
    <!-- include the Tools -->
    <script src=
    "http://ajax.googleapis.com/ajax/libs/jquery/1.6.4/jquery.min.js">
    </script>
    <script src=
      "http://cdn.jquerytools.org/1.2.6/all/jquery.tools.min.js">
    </script>
  </head>
  <body>
  </body>
</html>
```

Save this as a template—the demos in this book use a similar format, so this will help you save time later, when we look at some of the other tools available as part of the jQuery Tools UI library. Let's begin with overlays.

What is an overlay?

Overlays are a significant part of the JavaScript landscape—if you want to direct a visitor's attention to a specific element on your site, then this tool will achieve this to great effect. Overlays can be used to display virtually anything, such as different styles of overlays for displaying products, showing information or warning boxes, or to display complex information—these are all possible with jQuery Tools' Overlay.

Overlay for the perfect eye candy

jQuery Tools' Overlay can contain all sorts of information, such as videos, images, maps, and the like—everything can be styled using CSS. It has a variety of features, such as a scripting framework, event model (to perform an action when an event is triggered), as well as adding custom effects.

Usage

The general way to set up an overlay is as follows:

```
// select one or more elements to be overlay triggers
$(".my_overlay_trigger").overlay({

    // one configuration property
    color: '#ccc',

    // another property
    top: 50

    // ... the rest of the configuration properties
});
```

When you click on one of the triggers it will open an overlay that is being specified by the trigger's `rel` attribute.

 It is worth having a look at `http://flowplayer.org/tools/overlay/index.html`, which details all of the possible configuration options available for use with an overlay.

Let's see how this works in practice—we will build a simple map viewer that uses Google™ Maps, and the Apple effect from overlay.

Project: building a viewer for Google Maps

We're going to use this concept to develop a lightbox effect, which uses Google™ Maps, for a client who needs to provide a map of where his office is, but doesn't want to settle for a plain map on a page!

Creating the basic HTML structure

This example will use the Overlay tool from jQuery Tools, but with the "Apple" theme. All of the images used in the example are available in the code download that accompanies this book.

Remember the code template we set up at the beginning of this chapter? Grab a copy of it now and save this as your overlay project file, so that we can then add in the meat of the overlay demo. We will make one small change to it though—alter the `<body>` tags to read as this:

```
<body class="no-js">
...
</body>
```

The reasons for this will become clearer as we progress through the demonstration.

Adding in the overlay

Next, let's add the code for the overlay trigger and overlay to the `<body>`:

```
<!-- trigger elements -->
<a href="#link1" rel="#link1">Location of Packt's Office</a>

<!-- overlayed element -->
<div class="apple_overlay" id="link1">
  <iframe width="675" height="480" frameborder="0" scrolling="no"
          marginheight="0" marginwidth="0"
          src="http://maps.google.co.uk/maps?q=B3+2PB&amp;hl=en&amp;
sll=52.483277,-1.900152&amp;sspn=0.003679,0.009645&amp;vpsrc=0&amp;
t=m&amp;ie=UTF8&amp;hq=&amp;hnear=Birmingham,+West+Midlands+B3+2PB,
+United+Kingdom&amp;ll=52.484296,-1.90115&amp;
spn=0.015681,0.025749&amp;z=14&amp;iwloc=A&amp;output=embed">
  </iframe>
  <p>Packt's office in Birmingham</p>
</div>
```

This follows the normal overlay and trigger structure required for an overlay, but with the addition of the `<iframe>` markup, to handle external content. The trigger here is the `<a>` markup which, when clicked, opens the map showing the location of Packt's office and displays it in the overlay.

Setting up and configuring the overlay JavaScript

The next part to add in is the all-important script—although the code that calls the overlay functionality is only one line, we have to add a block of configuration code that tells it to use expose to hide the page contents, then show the overlay itself, and finally to find the URL given in the overlay HTML, and show this on screen.

Add the following code at the bottom of your web page, before the `</body>` tag:

```
<script>
$(function() {

    $("a[rel][href!='']").overlay({

        // some mask tweaks suitable for modal dialogs
        mask: {
            color: '#000',
            loadSpeed: 200,
            opacity: 0.8
        },
```

```
        effect: 'apple',

        onBeforeLoad: function() {
            var overlaid = this, overEl = this.getOverlay();

            // grab wrapper element inside content
            overEl.find(".contentWrap").load(
                    this.getTrigger().attr("href"));

            overEl.appendTo("body");
            $(".close", this.getOverlay()).click(function(e){
                overlaid.close();
            });
        }

    });
});
</script>
```

Adding the styling and visual effects

Finally, we need to add some styling, as the resulting page won't look very pretty!
The following code is crucial for showing the overlay, you can always change the
backgrounds being used, if you want to have a different color of overlay:

```
<style>
  /* body, a:active and : focus only needed for demo; these
     can be removed for production use */

  body { padding: 50px 80px; }
  a:active { outline: none; }
  :focus { -moz-outline-style: none; }

  .apple_overlay {

    /* initially overlay is hidden */
    display: none;

    /* growing background image */
    background-image: url(white.png);

    /* width after animation - height is auto-calculated */
    width: 675px;

    /* some padding to layout nested elements nicely  */
    padding: 25px;

    margin: 20px;
  }
```

```
/* default close button positioned on upper right corner */
.apple_overlay .close {
  background-image: url(close.png);
  position: absolute;
  right: -10px;
  top: -10px;
  cursor: pointer;
  height: 35px;
  width: 35px;
}

#overlay {
  height: 526px;
  width: 675px;
}

div.contentWrap {
  height: 526px;
  width: 675px;
  overflow: hidden;
}

a, body {
  font-family: Arial, Tahoma, Times New Roman;
}

body.no-js a[rel] {
  /* initially overlay is hidden if JavaScript is disabled */
  display: none;
}
body.js .apple_overlay {
  /* initially overlay is hidden if JavaScript is enabled */
  display: none;
}
</style>
```

 It is worth noting that if you want to change the background, there are some additional backgrounds available from the jQuery Tools website at http://flowplayer.org/tools/overlay/ index.html, or in the code download that accompanies this book. You can always add your own instead—have a look at some of the demos on the site to see how to do this.

Notice how we used `no-js` in the original HTML markup? The reason for this is simple: it maintains progressive enhancement, which means that if someone has JavaScript turned off, the overlay will still be hidden until you click on the trigger link!

The overlay will work now, you will see something similar to the following image:

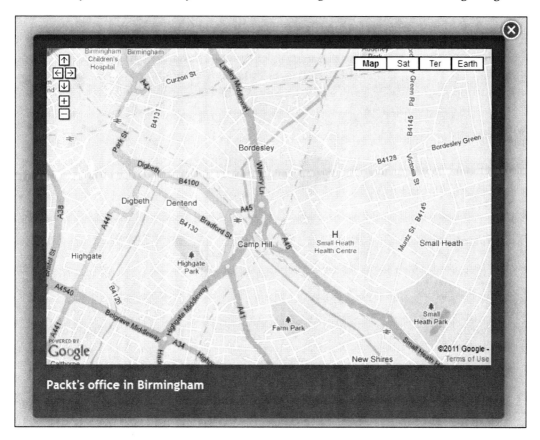

This only scratches the surface of what can be done with an overlay. You could add your own custom effects, set to show as a modal dialog, or even show different images as your "overlay", which could be enlarged versions of smaller images, such as a book.

Tooltips – the only web fundamentals you need

Arguably the second most important UI widget, the tooltip serves a similar purpose to the overlay, in that it can be used to highlight important pieces of information which relates to an element on screen, such as hints on how to fill in a form, a quicklink prompt to purchasing something, or highlighting information about a concept being discussed on site (in a similar fashion to having footnotes in a book). jQuery Tools' Tooltip is no different in operation to others, but its design makes it very powerful and flexible. Let's have a look at it in a little more detail.

Usage

Tooltips are very easy to set up, the basic version uses the folowing structure:

```
<!-- elements with tooltips -->
<div id="demo">
  <img src="image1.jpg" title="The tooltip text #1"/>
  <img src="image2.jpg" title="The tooltip text #2"/>
  <img src="image3.jpg" title="The tooltip text #3"/>
  <img src="image4.jpg" title="The tooltip text #4"/>
</div>
```

The trick to note with tooltips is that you can generate them in one of two ways, by using the `title` attribute or by including the tooltip block directly after the tooltip trigger.

 Tooltips that just need to display normal text are best achieved by using the [title] attribute. If you need to display more, or include HTML formatting, then use the manual method, with an individual CSS style class or ID selector.

Calling a tooltip can be as easy as simply using the selector element, which is normally the [title] attribute, which contains the text displayed as the tooltip:

```
$("[title]").tooltip();
```

If you need to display HTML elements, then you can use the manual format, which can contain any amount of HTML, but will use the element immediately after the trigger instead:

```
$(".trigger").tooltip();
```

We can take this even further by adding in some additional options—the slide and dynamic plugins.

 Using the [title] attribute on its own is not advisable; this will cause a performance hit as jQuery Tools will need to iterate through each instance to see if it should be converted to a tooltip. It is strongly recommended that a style class or ID should be used to improve performance.

Impress everyone with slide effect and dynamic plugins

The standard Tools' tooltips will serve a purpose, but have at least one inherent limitation—what happens if the browser window is resized? The tooltip doesn't allow for this by default, unless you add in the "dynamic" plugin, the dynamic plugin takes into account where the edges of the viewport are, and "dynamically" positions the tooltip accordingly. For extra functionality, you can also get the tooltip to slide in from the top, left, right, or bottom, rather than just appear in the same direction (from bottom to top). There are more details on the site on how to set up this additional feature.

In the meantime, let's have a look at a project that wouldn't be out of place on a website belonging to a bookshop or publisher, where you can use a "quicklink" to get more information and prices on a book, as well as buy a copy.

Project: building a book "buy now" using tooltip

You know the drill, you surf to a website where you see a book you want. You don't want to drill down lots of pages, just to buy it, right? I thought so—enter the Tooltip "quicklink". We're going to build in a little tooltip that pops up when you hover over a book, so that you can hit the **Buy** button directly.

 All of the images are available as part of the code download that accompanies the book, or can be obtained directly from the jQuery Tools website.

Setting up the basic HTML

Go grab a copy of the HTML template we set up at the beginning of this chapter, so that we can then copy in the basic trigger and tooltip HTML required to make this work:

```
<!-- trigger element. a regular workable link -->
<a id="download_now"><img src="book.jpg"></a>

<!-- tooltip element -->
<div class="tooltip">

  <img src="book.jpg" />

  <p class="bookavail">Book and eBook available now</p>

  <dl>
    <dt class="label">Book only price:</dt>
    <dt class="price">£25.19 save 10%</dt>

    <dt class="label">eBook only price:</dt>
    <dt class="price">£16.14 save 15%</dt>

    <dt class="buynow"><a href="/store/purchase?id=12345">
      <img src="buy_button.png"></a>
    </dt>
  </dl>
</div>
```

It's worth noting that, although the code isn't connected to an e-commerce system, you can easily adapt it:

```
<tr>
  <td></td>
  <td><a href="/store/purchase?id=12345">
      <img src="buy_button.png" /></a></td>
</tr>
```

Adding in the tooltip CSS styles

Now, here comes the crucial part—the styling. jQuery Tools follow the principle of minimal JavaScript coding, preferring to let most of the work be done by CSS. The Tooltip feature is no different, so let's add it to the code below the <head> section, to see the tooltip work:

```
<style>
  .tooltip { display: none; background: url(black_big.png);
            height: 145px; padding: 35px 30px 10px 30px;
```

```
                  width: 310px; font-size: 11px; color: #fff; }

   .tooltip img { float: left; margin: 0 5px 10px 0; }

   .bookavail { margin-top: -5px; color: #f00; font-weight: bold;
              font-size: 14px; }

   dt.label { float: left; font-weight: bold; width: 100px; }

   dt.price { margin-left: 210px; }

   dt.buynow a img { margin-top: 10px; margin-left: 110px; }
</style>
```

 It is important to note that the `.tooltip` class provides the base CSS required for any Tooltip to work; the rest of the CSS is specific to this demonstration.

We need some more styles though..!

Whilst the styles above will produce a workable demo, the presentation will not be perfect; we need to add additional styles to tweak the positioning of some of the elements, and fine tune the overall view. Add the following to your earlier stylesheet:

```
body { margin-top: 100px; margin-left: 200px; }

#booktip img { padding: 10px; opacity: 0.8;
             filter: alpha(opacity=80); -moz-opacity: 0.8; }

.bookavail { margin-top: -5px; color: #f00; font-weight: bold;
           font-size: 14px; }
```

Configuring the Tooltip

Last but by no means least, here's the JavaScript code required for the Tooltip to work. This is split into three parts:

- The first part configures the tooltip appearance on screen

- The second controls the fade in and out of the tooltip

- The final part adjusts the position of the tooltip on screen, to allow for the current browser window dimensions (that is, if it has been resized or is being displayed in full)

```
<script>
  $(document).ready(function() {
```

```
$("#booktip").tooltip({
  effect: 'slide',
  position: 'top right',
  relative: true,

  // change trigger opacity slowly to 1.0
  onShow: function() {
    this.getTrigger().fadeTo("slow", 1.0);
  },

  // change trigger opacity slowly to 0.8
  onHide: function() {
    this.getTrigger().fadeTo("slow", 0.8);
  }
}).dynamic({ bottom: { direction: 'down', bounce: true }});
});
</script>
```

For a simple project, the effect can be very striking—here's how it should look:

You can really go to town on the effects when using Tooltip—one such effect I have seen in use is that of a `div` that slides out, when hovering over an image; it may seem a little strange, but if you think about it, it is the same effect as used here. It still uses the Tooltip functionality from the Tools library, the only difference (which highlights the true power of jQuery Tools), is the CSS styling used!

For everything else – there's Scrollable

If you have a need to scroll through information on your site, then you will want to take a look at another component available within jQuery Tools: Scrollable. This tool can be used in many different ways, such as video galleries, product catalogues and news tickers—the structure is essentially the same throughout, but jQuery Tools' flexibility allows you to produce different designs, using the power of CSS.

Usage

This is the basic structure of Scrollable:

```
<!-- "previous page" action -->
<a class="prev browse left">next</a>
<!-- root element for scrollable -->
<div class="scrollable">
  <!-- root element for the items -->
  <div class="items">

    <!-- 1-3 -->
    <div>
      <img src="image1.jpg" />
      <img src="image2.jpg" />
      <img src="image3.jpg" />
    </div>

    <!-- 4-6 -->
    <div>
      <img src="image4.jpg" />
      <img src="image5.jpg" />
      <img src="image6.jpg" />
    </div>

    <!-- 7-9 -->
    <div>
      <img src="image7.jpg" />
      <img src="image8.jpg" />
      <img src="image9.jpg" />
    </div>
  </div>
</div>

<!-- "next page" action -->
<a class="next browse right">previous</a>
```

You will see that the structure is made up of a number of images grouped together, encased in a number of div tags, with additional div tags to look after the navigation elements. Although the demo only shows three images per group, you can easily add more images to each group, if desired.

To really show how this could work, let's have a look at an example, which would not be out of place on a hypothetical client's site, such as that of a photographer.

Project: building a mini gallery

The client has a number of images which need to be displayed on his site—he wants to be able to scroll through each group of images, and then click on one to show it in an enlarged viewer. Sounds simple enough, huh?

Setting up the basic HTML

To get started, let's put together the basic HTML structure. Open up your favorite text editor, and paste in the following:

```
<html>
  <head>
  </head>
  <body>
    <div id="swapframe">
      <div id="viewer">
        <div class="loadingspin">
          <img src="loadinfo.gif" alt="Loading..." />
        </div>
      </div>
      <div id="caption">x</div>
      <div id="scrollablecontainer">
        <a class="prev browse left"></a>
        <div id="overscroll">
          <div class="items">
            <div class="item">
              <div>
                <a rel="odontoglossum"
                   href="images/odontoglossum.jpg">
                  <img src="thumbnails/odontoglossum_tn.jpg"
                       align="middle" />
                </a>
              </div>
              <div>
                <a rel="forest orchid"
```

```
            href="images/forest%2520orchid.jpg">
          <img src="thumbnails/forest%2520orchid_tn.jpg"
              align="middle" />
      </a>
    </div>
    <div>
      <a rel="brassia" href="images/brassia.jpg">
        <img src="thumbnails/brassia_tn.jpg"
            align="middle" />
      </a>
    </div>
    <div>
      <a rel="paphiopedilum"
        href=" images/paphiopedilum.jpg">
        <img src="thumbnails/paphiopedilum_tn.jpg"
            align="middle" />
      </a>
    </div>
    <div>
      <a rel="zygopetalum"
        href=" images/zygopetalum.jpg">
        <img src="thumbnails/zygopetalum_tn.jpg"
            align="middle" />
      </a>
    </div>
  </div>
  <div class="item">
    <div>
      <a rel="cactus flower"
        href=" images/cactus%2520flower.jpg">
        <img src="thumbnails/cactus%2520flower_tn.jpg"
            align="middle" />
      </a>
    </div>
    <div>
      <a rel="african violet"
        href=" images/african%2520violet.jpg">
        <img src="thumbnails/african%2520violet_tn.jpg"
            align="middle" />
      </a>
    </div>
    <div>
      <a rel="pink camelia"
```

```
                    href=" images/pink%2520camelia.jpg ">
                    <img src="thumbnails/pink%2520camelia_tn.jpg"
                            align="middle" />
                </a>
            </div>
            <div>
                <a rel="red camelia"
                    href=" images/red%2520camelia.jpg ">
                    <img src="thumbnails/red%2520camelia_tn.jpg"
                            align="middle" />
                </a>
            </div>
            <div>
                <a rel="white camelia"
                    href=" images/white%2520camelia.jpg ">
                    <img src="thumbnails/white%2520camelia_tn.jpg"
                            align="middle" />
                </a>
            </div>
            </div>
          </div>
        </div>
        <a class="next browse right"></a>
      </div>
    </div>
  </body>
</html>
```

In previous examples, we used the template file that we created at the beginning of this chapter. This time around, I've provided the whole example, as there is some additional HTML included here. I've included a loading animated GIF, as well as space for an image caption.

It looks complicated, but in reality it isn't—it's following the same structure shown above, but has a number of additional DIVs enclosing the HTML code; this is largely to allow us to position the results on screen correctly, while still maintaining each element in the right place .

Time for some JavaScript magic

Okay, now that we have the structure in place, let's add in the JavaScript code. Copy in these two lines into your `<head>` area:

```
<script src=
    "http://ajax.googleapis.com/ajax/libs/jquery/1.6.4/jquery.min.js">
```

```
</script>
<script src=
   "http://cdn.jquerytools.org/1.2.6/all/jquery.tools.min.js">
</script>
```

This initiates the calls to the jQuery and jQuery Tools libraries, so you can start to use both. Here comes the critical part of this example, which you can copy in just below the previous lines:

```
<script>
$(function(){
  $.ajaxSetup({
    cache: false,
    dataType: "text html"
  });

  $(".loadingspin").bind('ajaxStart', function(){
    $(this).show();
  }).bind('ajaxComplete', function(){
    $(this).hide();
  });

  $.fn.loadimage = function(src, f){
    return this.each(function(){
      $("<img />").attr("src", src).appendTo(this).each(function(){
        this.onload = f;
      });
    });
  }

  $(".item img:first").load(function(){
    var firstpic = $(".item a:first").attr("rel");
    $("#caption").text(firstpic);
    $("#viewer").empty().loadimage("images/" + firstpic +
              ".jpg").hide().fadeIn('fast');
  });

  $(".item a").unbind('click.pic').bind('click.pic', function(e){
    e.preventDefault();
    var picindex = $(this).attr("rel");
    $("#caption").text(picindex);
    $("#viewer").empty().loadimage("images/" + picindex +
              ".jpg").hide().fadeIn('fast');
  });

  $("#overscroll").scrollable();

  $("a.browse").click(function(){
```

```
        $("#swapframe").load("ajax/" + state +
                        ".html").hide().fadeIn('fast');
    });
</script>
```

This code provides the gallery and scrollable effect, it loads in each image as you click on the thumbnail in the Scrollable. You can even add in an option effect that fades out images, if you are hovering over one:

```
<script type="text/javascript">
$(function(){
    $('.item').children().hover(function() {
        $(this).siblings().stop().fadeTo(500,0.5);
    }, function() {
        $(this).siblings().stop().fadeTo(500,1);
    });
});
```

Time for some styles

If you try to run the previous code, it will work, but will look terrible—there will be missing images, and you won't be able to navigate through the Scrollable, for example. This is where the true power of jQuery Tools comes into play, most of the real work is actually done in the CSS styling:

```
<style>
  #scrollablecontainer { position: relative; top: -30px;
                        height: 52px; }

  /* prev, next, up and down buttons */
  a.browse { background:url(hori_large.png) no-repeat;
            display: block; float: left; width: 30px; height: 30px;
            float: left; margin: 10px; cursor: pointer;
            font-size: 1px;
          }

  /* right */
  a.right { background-position: 0 -30px; clear: right;
          margin-right: 0px;}
  a.right:hover { background-position: -30px -30px; }
  a.right:active { background-position: -60px -30px; }

  /* left */
  a.left { margin-left: 0; }
  a.left:hover { background-position: -30px 0; }
  a.left:active { background-position: -60px 0; }
```

```
/* disabled navigational button */
a.disabled { visibility: hidden !important; }

#overscroll { position: relative; float: left; width:
            550px; height: 50px; border: 1px solid #ccc;
            overflow: hidden; }

.items { position: absolute; clear: both; width: 20000em; }
.item { float: left; width: 550px; }
.item div { float: left; width: 100px; height: 40px;
           margin: 5px; background: #ccc; }
</style>
```

These styles are crucial for setting up basic effects, such as providing navigation buttons and the scrollable container.

Some extra styling

However, it could use some additional tweaks to make it really stand out. Let's add those in now:

```
<link href=
  'http://fonts.googleapis.com/css?family=Cedarville+Cursive'
  rel='stylesheet' type='text/css'>

<style>
  #swapframe { height: 540px; width: 640px;
            padding: 25px 25px 0 20px; margin: 0 auto;
            background: transparent url(slideshow-bg.gif)
            no-repeat; background-size: 680px 540px;}

  #viewer { height: 355px; background: #000; }

  .loadingspin { float: center; margin-top: auto;
              margin-bottom: auto; }

  #caption { position: relative; top: -10px; width: 200px;
           margin: 0 auto; color: #000; text-align: center;
           font-size: 30px; font-family: 'Cedarville Cursive',
           cursive; padding-bottom: 35px; }
</style>
```

The code will transform the gallery into something useable; it even includes a handwritten font for the caption, which uses Google™ Fonts. If all is well, you should see something like the following:

This is just a small part of what you can do with Scrollable. You can go further, or even combine Scrollable with other elements of Tools, such as an Overlay, which would show a really impressive effect!

Tabs in action

It's time to take a look at the fourth and final part of the UI Tools section of jQuery Tools—that of Tabs.

Tabs can be described as one of the most popular user interfaces on the Internet. This is for good reason since they are easy to use and contain lots of information in a confined space, which you can then organize in a more user-friendly manner. Let's have a look at them in a little more detail.

Usage

The basic structure of Tabs is as follows:

```
<!-- the tabs -->
<ul class="tabs">
  <li><a href="#">Tab 1</a></li>
```

```
  <li><a href="#">Tab 2</a></li>
  <li><a href="#">Tab 3</a></li>
</ul>

<!-- tab "panes" -->
<div class="panes">
  <div>pane 1 content</div>
  <div>pane 2 content</div>
  <div>pane 3 content</div>
</div>
```

These would then be activated as Tabs, by using the following JavaScript call:

```
$("ul.tabs").tabs("div.panes > div");
```

But, hold on; isn't this the basic code for Scrollable? Well, yes, there are some similarities. But no, this is definitely the code for Tabs! There are some similarities between the two tools, but it is important to note that they are not interchangeable.

This said, it's time to start building our next project.

Project: building a rolling slideshow

We're going to use the power of Tab's Slideshow plugin, to build a demo that could be used on a photo gallery website. It's a slideshow styled as a Polaroid, but with some additional functionality. It will use similar images to the Scrollable, but in a different format—one that can easily be put on most websites. Similar effects are used by some well-known companies with an Internet presence.

Setting up the basic HTML

To begin with, let's get out our text editor. Grab a copy of the template code from the start of this chapter, and add the following lines to create the HTML base:

```
<div id="caption"></div>
<!-- container for the slides -->
<div class="images">
  <div>
    <img class="slides" src="images/odontoglossum.jpg"
         rel="odontoglossum" />
  </div>
  <div>
    <img class="slides" src="images/forest orchid.jpg"
         rel="forest orchid" />
  </div>
```

```
<div>
  <img class="slides" src="images/brassia.jpg"
       rel="brassia" />
</div>
<div>
  <img class="slides" src="images/paphiopedilum.jpg"
       rel="paphiopedilum" />
</div>
</div>

<div id="galprevnext">
  <div class="galleft">
    <a class="galprevpic hideit"></a>
  </div>

  <div class="galright">
    <a class="galnextpic hideit"></a>
  </div>
</div>

<!-- the tabs -->
<div class="slidetabs">
  <a href="#">1</a>
  <a href="#">2</a>
  <a href="#">3</a>
  <a href="#">4</a>
</div>

<div id="playcontrols">
  <img src="play.gif" />
  <img src="stop.gif" />
</div>
```

This can be broken down into five distinct sections, namely the header, the container for the pictures, the gallery controls, the tabs, and finally the player controls.

Adding the visual effects

The next section is the all-important styling—this comes in two parts, beginning with the compulsory code for the Polaroid effect and the slideshow:

```
<link href=
  'http://fonts.googleapis.com/css?family=Cedarville+Cursive'
  rel='stylesheet' type='text/css'>
```

```css
<style type="text/css">

 body { padding-left:400px; padding-top: 50px; }

 /* container for slides */
 .images { border: 1px solid #ccc; position: relative;
          height: 450px; width: 502px; float: left; margin: 15px;
          cursor: pointer;

          /* CSS3 tweaks for modern browsers */
          -moz-border-radius: 5px;
          -webkit-border-radius: 5px;
          border-radius: 5px;
          -moz-box-shadow: 0 0 25px #666;
          -webkit-box-shadow: 0 0 25px #666;
          box-shadow: 0 0 25px #666; }

 /* single slide */
 .images div { display: none; position: absolute; top: 0; left: 0;
              margin: 3px; padding: 15px 30px 15px 15px;
              height: 256px; font-size: 12px; }

 /* tabs (those little circles below slides) */
 .slidetabs { position: absolute; margin: 350px 600px 0 440px;
             width: 100px; }

 /* single tab */
 .slidetabs a { width: 8px; height: 8px; float: left; margin: 3px;
               background: url(navigator.png) 0 0 no-repeat;
               display: block; font-size: 1px; color: #fff; }

 /* mouseover state */
 .slidetabs a:hover { background-position: 0 -8px; }

 /* active state (current page state) */
 .slidetabs a.current { background-position: 0 -16px; }

 /* prev and next buttons */
 .forward, .backward { float: left; margin-top: 120px;
                      background: #fff url(nav.png) no-repeat;
                      width: 35px;         height: 35px;
                      cursor: pointer; z-index: 2; }

 /* next */
 .forward { background-position: -36px 0px ; }
 .forward:hover,
 .forward:active { background-position: -36px -36px; }
```

```
/* prev */
.backward:hover,
.backward:active { background-position: 0 -36px; }

/* disabled navigational button. is not needed when tabs
   are configured with rotate: true */
.disabled { visibility: hidden !important; }

#caption { color: black; margin-left: 35px; margin-top: 345px;
           position: absolute; width: 200px;
           font-family: 'Cedarville Cursive', cursive;
           font-size: 26px; }

.slides { border-width: 0; height:310px; width:466px; }
</style>
```

Phew, there's a lot of style code there! Most of it relates to positioning the slides, as well as providing the navigator buttons and caption.

> You will see the real power of CSS styling here, as the Polaroid effect is generated entirely using CSS3 code; it is for this reason it won't look so spectacular in older browsers. However jQuery Tools is about using HTML5 (and CSS3), and less for older browsers. You could still get around this by adding the appropriate styles for a suitable background image if desired.

"Mmm…I want more!"

When it came to writing the project for this book, I wasn't entirely happy—I wanted more. It took a little rearranging and tweaking, but finally with some help from a fellow user of jQuery Tools, Mudimo, I managed to put together a little something extra, based on one of his excellent demos.

The first part is to add some buttons to control the slideshow, which replace the standard ones that could be added, that are available from the jQuery Tools site. Add the following in as an additional set of styles:

```
<style>
#galprevnext { position: absolute; width: 640px; height: 539px; }

.galleftpic, .galrightpic { width: 270px; height: 539px;
                            cursor: pointer; }

.galleftpic { float: left; }

.galrightpic { float: right; }
```

```
.galprevpic, .galnextpic { display: block; position: absolute;
                           top: 140px; width: 30px; height: 30px;
                           margin: 0 10px; }

.galprevpic { float: left; background: url(prevnext.png) 0 0
              no-repeat; margin-left: 9px; }

.galnextpic { float: right; background: url(prevnext.png)
              -30px 0 no-repeat; margin-left: 100px; }

.hideit { visibility: hidden; cursor: arrow; }

.showit { visibility: visible; cursor: pointer; }

#galprevnext a { text-decoration: none; }

#galprevnext a:hover { color: #f00; }

#galprevnext a.current { color: #00f; }

#galprevnext .disabled { visibility: hidden; }

.galleft, .galright { height: 310px; margin-top: 35px;
                      position: absolute; width: 150px; }
.galleft { margin-left: 35px; }
.galright { margin-left: 360px; }

#playcontrols { clear: both; margin-left: 375px;
                margin-top: 350px; padding-right: 40px;
                position: absolute; }
</style>
```

You'll notice that this tries where possible to keep to the standards of abstracting images out of the main code, which is one of the main tenets of jQuery Tools. The second part of his code was to add a little additional jQuery, which alters the CSS style of `hideit` to `showit` and back again, depending on whether the mouse is hovering over either of the buttons (the two styles control visibility of the buttons). As a final tweak, we add some additional styling to the player controls, by replacing the original buttons with styled icons, and using a little CSS to place these next to the navigator "dots" just below the pictures.

Configuring the Tab effects

We move onto the final part of the code, which is to add in the JavaScript required to make this all work. Add this at the bottom of your page:

```
$(function() {

  $(".slidetabs").tabs(".images > div", {

    // enable "cross-fading" effect
```

```
  effect: 'fade',
  fadeOutSpeed: "slow",

  // start from the beginning after the last tab
  rotate: true,

  // here is a callback function that is called before the
  // tab is clicked
  onClick: function(event, tabIndex) {
    var str = $("img").eq(tabIndex).attr("rel");
    $("#caption").html(str);
  }

  // use the slideshow plugin, which has its own config
})
.slideshow({
  prev: ".galleft",
  next: ".galright"
});
});
```

This is the all-important part of the code—it configures the Tabs effect to use the slideshow plugin, and extract the text from the `rel` tag in the code, which is used as the caption. Note how, as the next and back buttons use non-default CSS class names, these need to be set in the configuration options for the slideshow plugin, so it knows how to operate correctly.

Setting the button visibility

Remember the two buttons I decided to add in earlier, as extras? The next two sections of code achieve two goals; the first controls the visibility of those two buttons, the second allows you to stop and start the slideshow.

If we take a look at the first section, which controls the visibility—jQuery changes the style from `hideit` to `showit`, which in turn alters the visibility from hidden to visible and back again, when hovering over either of the buttons:

```
$(".galleft").mouseover(function(){
    $(".galprevpic").removeClass('hideit').addClass('showit');
}).mouseout(function(){
    $(".galprevpic").removeClass('showit').addClass('hideit');
});

$(".galright").mouseover(function(){
    $(".galnextpic").removeClass('hideit').addClass('showit');
}).mouseout(function(){
    $(".galnextpic").removeClass('showit').addClass('hideit');
});
```

We then need to be able to control the playback of the slideshow. We can do this by adding event handlers to both image buttons, like so:

```
$("#playbutton").click(function(){
    $(".slidetabs").data("slideshow").play();
});

$("#stopbutton").click(function(){
    $(".slidetabs").data("slideshow").stop();
});
```

And there you have it, if all is well, you should have something looking like the following screenshot. The tools available in jQuery Tools are all infinitely customizable, this demo is just one small example of what we can possibly achieve within the confines of this book:

Summary

In this chapter, we looked at some examples of what is possible with the main components of jQuery Tools, namely Scrollable, Overlay, Tooltips, and Tabs. All are infinitely customizable, the examples discussed in the chapter outline how, while the basic functionality of each tool may be minimal, the overall architecture of each tool allows for heavy customization using CSS as desired, and hopefully it has given you some inspiration for your own projects.

Now that we've learned about the four main tools, it is time to turn our attention to the second group of tools available as part of the Tools Library, namely Validator, DateInput, and RangeInput, which will be the subject of the next chapter.

3
Form Tools

Ask yourself a question: do you like filling in forms? If, as I suspect, the answer is no, then join the masses — there is nothing worse than filling in a form online, only to find you've entered in something incorrectly, and you have to go back and change it…

Enter jQuery Tools' Form Tools!

This group of 3 useful tools may not be as popular as some of the other tools in the library, but they still serve a useful function.

In this chapter we will learn about the following:

- How to use Validator to ensure a form is correctly filled out, or to display errors when this is not the case
- How to update the basic style of DateInput, using elements of jQuery UI's themes
- How to turn RangeInput into a browser, so you can scroll through a number of products, and some tips on how to combine it with other tools

So…what are you waiting for? Let's get started with looking at Validator.

Using Validator

Validators can be used to ensure whether a form is correctly filled out. Validators can also be used to display the errors.

Why basic Validator?

The art of form filling, as defined by Wikipedia, means that you cannot simply submit forms with any old rubbish, or saying "put rubbish in, and you get rubbish out" will definitely be true. It is crucial to ensure that the content you enter at least conforms to some form of minimum standard — one of the tools that can help with this is Validator. Let's have a look at this component of the Tools library in a little more detail.

 Data validation is the process of ensuring that a program operates on clean, correct and useful data.

Usage

The basic code for Validator is in two parts — the first part is the HTML structure, with the second part a single line call to the Validator tool:

```
<form id="myform" novalidate="novalidate">
  <fieldset>
    <h3>Sample registration form</h3>
    <p> Enter bad values and then press the submit button. </p>
    <p>
    <label>email *</label>
      <input type="email" name="email" required="required" />
    </p>
    <p>
    <label>website *</label>
      <input type="url" name="url" required="required" />
    </p>
    <p>
    <label>name *</label>
      <input type="text" name="name" pattern="[a-zA-Z ]{5,}"
      maxlength="30" />
    </p>
    <p>
    <label>age</label>
      <input type="number" name="age" size="4" min="5" max="50" />
    </p>
    <p id="terms">
      <label>I accept the terms</label>
      <input type="checkbox" required="required" />
    </p>
```

```
        <button type="submit">Submit form</button>
        <button type="reset">Reset</button>
    </fieldset>
</form>
```

Once you have the form set up, then you need to add the call for Validator—here's the basic code:

```
$("#myform").validator();
```

 Notice that this includes the `novalidate` attribute on the form—this is to force IE not to try to use the HTML5 validator that works in more modern browsers, but to use that from jQuery Tools instead.

With this in mind, let's put it into practice, by setting up a demonstration of how we can use Validator in a form.

Project: improving styling, and adding custom field validators

We're going to use an existing form, available from the jQuery Tools site, and add some tweaks in the form of additional validators, and changes to the configuration.

Creating the basic HTML structure

Open up the text editor of your choice, and copy in the following code—you will notice that it follows a similar pattern to most of the projects in this book:

```
<!DOCTYPE html>
<html>
  <head>
  <title>jQuery Tools standalone demo</title>
    <!-- include the Tools -->
    <script src="http://cdn.jquerytools.org
    /1.2.6/full/jquery.tools.min.js"></script>
  </head>
  <body>
  </body>
</html>
```

Adding in the form details

Okay. Now we have the basic structure in place, let's start filling it out with a little detail. First up is the form content, with the fields that we are going to validate—so copy in the code below in between the `<body>` tags:

```
<form id="myform">
  <fieldset>
    <h3>Sample registration form</h3>
      <span class="errorlabel">Oops - it seems there are some errors!
      Please check and correct them.</span>

      <p> Enter bad values and then press the submit button. </p>

      <p>
        <label>email *</label>
        <input type="email" name="email" id="email"
        required="required" />
      </p>
      <p>
        <label>website *</label>

        <input type="url" name="url" required="required" />
      </p>
      <p>
        <label>name *</label>
        <input type="text" name="name" pattern="[a-zA-Z ]{5,}"
        maxlength="30" />
      </p>
      <p>
        <label>time *</label>
        <input type="time" name="time" required="required" data-
        message="Please enter a valid time"/>
      </p>
      <p>
        <label>age</label>
        <input type="number" name="age" size="4" min="5" max="50" />
      </p>
      <p>
        <label>password</label>
        <input type="password" name="password" minlength="4" />
      </p>
      <p>
        <label>password check</label>
```

```
        <input type="password" name="check" data-equals="password" />
      </p>
      <p>
        <label>filename *</label>
        <input type="file" name="uploadfile" required="required" />
      </p>
      <p>
        <input type="phone" name="phone" data-message="Please
        enter a valid US telephone number." required="required"
        pattern="(?:1-?)?(d{3})[-.]?(d{3})[-.]?(d{4})" />
      </p>
      <p>
        <label>Gender</label>
        <select value="" required="required" name="sex">
          <option></option>
          <option value="male">Male</option>
          <option value="female">Female</option>
      </select>
      </p>
      <p id="terms">
        <label>I accept the terms</label>
        <input type="checkbox" required="required" />
      </p>
    <button type="submit">Submit form</button>
    <button type="reset" id="clearform">Reset</button>
  </fieldset>
</form>
```

 Notice that there are a number of additional parameters that pop up in the code, such as the pattern attribute in the Telephone input field. These are used by Validator and/or its additional custom validators, as a basis for validating text entered by the person visiting the site.

Styling the form

Now that is done, we need to add in the all important styling—note that this does include some additional styles for the purposes of this demo, but are not necessarily required in your live projects:

```
<style>
/* body, a:active and : focus only needed for demo; these can be
removed for production use */
  body { padding: 50px 80px; }
  a:active { outline: none; }
```

```
:focus { -moz-outline-style: none; }
/* form style */
#myform { background: #333 0 0; padding: 15px 20px; color:
#eee; width: 440px; margin: 0 auto; position: relative;
  -moz-border-radius: 5px; -webkit-border-radius: 5px; border-
  radius: 5px; }
/* nested fieldset */
#myform fieldset { border: 0; margin: 0; padding: 0;
  background: #333 url(logo-medium.png) no-repeat scroll
  215px 40px; }
/* typography */
#myform h3 { color: #eee; margin-top: 0px; }
#myform p { font-size: 11px; }
/* input field */
#myform input { border: 1px solid #444; background-
  color: #666; padding: 5px; color: #ddd; font-size: 12px;
  text-shadow: 1px 1px 1px #000; -moz-border-radius: 4px;
  -webkit-border-radius: 4px; border-radius: 4px; }
/* take care here: support for :focus and :active limited in some
browsers! */
#myform input:focus { color: #fff; background-color: #777; }
#myform input:active { background-color: #888; }
/* button */
#myform button { outline: 0; border: 1px solid #666; }
/* error message */
  .error { font-size: 11px; color: #f00; display: none; }
  .error p { margin:15px; margin-left: 20px; font-weight: bold;
  background-color: #fff; -moz-border-radius:4px;
  -webkit-border-radius: 4px; padding: 2px; border-radius: 4px;}
/* field label */
  label { display:block; font-size:11px; color:#ccc; }
#terms label { float: left; }
#terms input { margin: 0 5px; }
  .invalid { -moz-box-shadow: 0 0 2px 2px #f00; -webkit-box-shadow:
  0 0 2px 2px #f00; box-shadow: 0 0 2px 2px #f00; }
  .errorlabel { display: none; font-size: 14px; font-weight: bold;
  color: #f00; }
  .error img { position: absolute; margin: 15px 15px 15px 0;}
  .errorhilite { border: 3px solid #f00; }
  </style>
</head>
```

The final part – the script

The final part required is the all important script, to make it all work – as this is a reasonably long script, we will break it down into sections, starting with the validators.

Custom Validators

While Validator will use standard HTML4 and HTML5 validators, the functionality only really comes into its own when you add in custom validators, that are not available as a part of the normal library. We have five examples of custom validators in this demo, so copy the following code into your site – this should be the last stage on your page, or in the <head> area, as long as the document.ready() function is used accordingly:

```
<script>
```

This validator performs a check on <select> drop downs:

```
// custom Validator for <select> dropdowns
$.tools.validator.fn("select", "Select a value", function(input,
value) {
  return (value == 'none') ? false : true;
});
```

If you want to use radio buttons, then this is the validator code you need to use:

```
// custom Validator for radio buttons
$.tools.validator.fn("[group-required]", "At least one option needs to
be selected.", function(input) {
  var name = input.attr("group-required");
  var group_members = $('input[name=' + name + ']');
  var checked_count = group_members.filter(':checked').length;
  if((checked_count == 0) && (group_members.first().attr('id') ==
input.attr('id'))) {
    $('input[name=' + name + ']').click(function() {
      validate_form.data("validator").reset($('input[name=' + name +
      ']'));
    });
    return false;
  } else {
    return true;
  }
});
```

The validator below will do a pattern match for a valid time:

```
// custom Validator for "time" input type
$.tools.validator.fn("[type=time]", function(el, value) {
  return /^(2[0-4]|[01]?\d):[0-6]\d$/.test(value) ? true : "Please
  provide a valid time, using military format";
});
```

This validator will flag an error if the minimum character length is not obeyed:

```
// custom alidator based on minimum required length
$.tools.validator.fn("[minlength]", function(input, value) {
  var min = input.attr("minlength");

  if (isNaN(min)) {
    return true; // not a valid minlength, so skip validation
  } else {
    return value.length >= min ? true : {
      en: "Please provide at least " +min+ "
      character" + (min > 1 ? "s" : ""),
      fi: "Kentän minimipituus on " +min+ " merkkiä"
    };
  }
});
```

This validator will show an error if the uploaded file type is not one of the pre-determined types:

```
// custom validator based on a required filetype
$.tools.validator.fn("[type=file]", "Please choose a file with an
allowed extensions", function(input, value) {
  if ($(":file").val() != "") {
    return /\.jpg\png\gif\pdf\doc\txt)$/.test(value);
  } else {
    return true;
  }
});
```

The real heart of the validator script is as given below, it contains the call to jQuery Tools' Validator functionality, with a number of additional configuration options. In order, they do the following:

- position: It controls the location on screen where the text will appear
- speed: It determines how fast or slow the error message appears
- offset: It is used in conjunction with position to fine-tune the location on screen

- errorClass and errorInputEvent: The CSS style to use on the error message, and the trigger for the input validity check

- message: The text of the error message, including any images (as shown here)

- inputEvent: It revalidates text each time the user "blurs" or moves away from the element—this is used particularly on the checking of <select> tags

Copy this into your script section:

```
$(document).ready(function () {
  $("#myform").validator({
    position: 'center right',
    speed: 'slow',
    offset: [0, 10],
    errorClass: 'invalid',
    errorInputEvent: 'keyup change',
    message: '<div><img src=images/exclamation.png></div>',
    inputEvent: "blur"
  });
})
```

This next section performs two functions – the first one is to set Validator to automatically reposition the error message text, if the window is resized; the second one adds a red border on fields that do not validate properly, on a trigger of "onFail", when the submit button is pressed:

```
// get handle to the Validator API
  var myForm = $("#myform"),
  api = myForm.data("validator");

    api.reflow();

    myForm.bind("onFail", function(e, errors)  {

    // we are only doing stuff when the form is submitted
    if (e.originalEvent.type == 'submit') {
    $(".errorlabel").css({ display: 'block'});

    // loop through Error objects and add the border color
      $.each(errors, function()  {
        var input = this.input;
          input.css( 'errorhilite' ).focus(function()  {
          input.css( 'errorhilite' );
      });
    });
  }
});
```

The final part of this script is a reset function that clears the red border set against any field that doesn't validate correctly:

```
$("#clearform").click(function() {
  myForm.reset();
  $(".errorlabel").css({ display: 'none' });

  // loop through Error objects and add the border color
  $("input, select").each(function(index) {
    $(this).css({ border: '' });
    });
  });
})
</script>
```

If all has worked correctly, then you should see something like the form shown in the next screenshot:

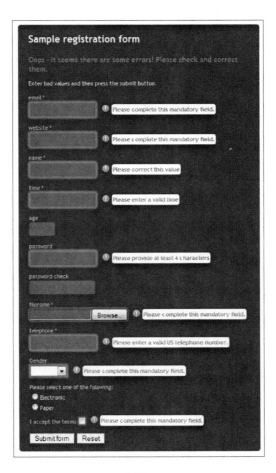

"It seems very negative, this onFail..."

Yes, it is true—a potential downside of Validator is that it does feel very one-sided in that it concentrates on only when input entries fail. However, it is possible to include code to display a confirmation or message if the validator deems that the entry concerned does match the required pattern.

 You should note that,this is a concept only at the moment; it is meant as a starting point for your own development, and would need thorough testing before putting into production use.

To do this, you can try the following:

1. Add the following into your style sheet:

```
input.valid {
    background-image: url(images/accept.png);
    background-position: right top;
    background-repeat: no-repeat;
}

input.valid.invalid {
    background-image: none;
}
```

2. Add this to your JavaScript call to jQuery:

```
// use API to assign an event listener
api.onSuccess(function(e, els) {
    $("input[required]").addClass('valid');

    // we don't want to submit the form. just show events.
    return false;
});
```

3. Add this to the bottom of your `reset` method:

```
$('input').removeClass("valid");
```

4. Add this line to the configuration set up for Validator:

```
errorInputEvent: 'keyup change',
```

The code is not perfect – it has some bugs in it, so should only be treated as a starting point for your own ideas. If you do implement the code above, then you should see something like the following screenshot:

Validator – a final thought

This demo scratches just the surface of what can be done with Validator – Validator will happily work with jQuery Tools' Overlay functionality, so that you could show the errors in a dialog box, with the overlay mask behind, for example. You can even use jQuery UI to provide that dialog box effect as well – the key to using jQuery UI is to declare the call to jQuery Tools first, then reassign the Tabs object in Tools to use a different naming convention, otherwise it will conflict with UI.

In the next section, we will take a look at another important tool in the library – DateInput.

Making your HTML5 date input look and behave the way you want with Dateinput

The advent of HTML5 has brought the ability to use `<input type=date>`, which removes the need for additional functionality. However, this is only available in a limited capacity, as it only works on Safari – jQuery Tools seeks to redress this with DateInput, which makes the HTML5 functionality available now, across all modern browsers. Let's take a peek at how to use it.

Usage

If there was an example of where minimal JavaScript was needed, then this is arguably one of them; DateInput only needs two words to work, with the exception of the call to the library, of course! Below is the basic framework required to get jQuery Tools' DateInput working:

```
<!-- include jQuery FORM Tools (or any other combination) -->
<script src="http://cdn.jquerytools.org/1.2.6/form/
jquery.tools.min.js">
```

```
</script>
<!-- dateinput styling -->
<link rel="stylesheet" type="text/css" href="dateinput.css"/>

<!-- HTML5 date input -->
<input type="date" />

<!-- make it happen -->
<script>
  $(":date").dateinput();
</script>
```

With this in mind, it's time to look at a project using DateInput – this time though, this will be a project with a difference.

Project: styling and localization

When preparing the demos for this book, I originally had in mind something that would try to showcase some of the functionality of DateInput. However, on reflection, I wanted to do something else, which was to answer the question – "is it possible to combine elements from jQuery UI's themes into jQuery Tools?"

The inspiration for this came from the themes that are available with jQuery UI—themes are one area where DateInput is lacking. In this project, we're going to look at styling DateInput using the original skin, but making a number of tweaks to first add some color and then localization.

Creating the basic HTML

To begin with, let's create the basic HTML structure – open up your text editor, and copy in the following lines as a starting point:

```
<!DOCTYPE html>
<html>
  <head>
    <title>jQuery Tools standalone demo</title>

    <!-- include the Tools -->
    <script src="http://cdn.jquerytools.org/1.2.6/full/
    jquery.tools.min.js"></script>

    <!-- standalone page styling (can be removed) -->
    <link rel="stylesheet" type="text/css" href="http://
    static.flowplayer.org/tools/css/standalone.css"/>
    <link rel="stylesheet" type="text/css" href="skin1.css">
```

```
      <style>
      </style>
    </head>

    <body>
      <!-- HTML5 date input -->
      <input type="date" name="mydate" data-value: "Today" />

      <!-- make it happen -->

      <script>
      </script>
    </body>

  </html>
```

Okay, there is nothing complicated here; save a copy of this as your base HTML file, ready for adding the CSS and JavaScript code. You will notice the similarities to other projects in this book, where minimal HTML is required to build a usable structure—DateInput is no different.

> Notice that the `<input type="date">` tag is used here—whilst this is valid HTML5, the beauty of jQuery Tools lies in making this available to all modern browsers, not just ones that accept HTML5. If JavaScript is not available for any reason, this will actually degrade nicely for those using Safari!

Setting up the JavaScript

Moving on, let's add in the JavaScript we're going to use for DateInput:

```
// the french localization
$.tools.dateinput.localize("fr",  {
  months: 'janvier,f&eacute;vrier,mars,avril,
  mai,juin,juillet,ao&ucirc;t,' +
  'septembre,octobre,novembre,d&eacute;cembre',
  shortMonths:   'jan,f&eacute;v,mar,avr,mai,jun,
  jul,ao&ucirc;,sep,oct,nov,d&eacute;c',
  days:          'dimanche,lundi,mardi,mercredi,
  jeudi,vendredi,samedi',
  shortDays:     'dim,lun,mar,mer,jeu,ven,sam'
});

$(":date").dateinput({
  format: 'dddd, ddth mmmm yyyy',
```

```
    lang: 'fr',
    offset: [0, 30],
    yearRange: [-20, 20]
});
```

This comes in two parts – the first part is the localization code for DateInput, which gives the French language equivalents for the months and days of the year. This is used by DateInput—to activate it, the `lang` attribute needs to be used, along with the correct two letter code for the appropriate language.

The second part of the code is the call to DateInput, where the format and desired language is specified (the latter using the same code from the localization code).

Adding the styling

This is arguably the most important part of DateInput – the styling. You will notice that the original `skin1.css` link has been included in the code at the beginning of this project; this is to illustrate that the original skin can be overridden, and that it is not necessary to always try to reinvent the wheel. You will also need to download the "Start" theme from the jQueryUI site at `http://www.jqueryui.com`; if using this styling technique, you will need to refer to this, to extract the relevant CSS that make up your custom styles. Copy the code given below into the style tags in your webpage:

```
// body, a:active and : focus only needed for demo; these can be
// removed for production use
    body { padding:50px 80px; }
    a:active { outline:none; }
    :focus { -moz-outline-style:none; }
    .date { width: 260px; }

#calroot { width:210px; }
#calhead { background: url("ui-bg_gloss-
wave_75_2191c0_500x100.png") repeat-x scroll 50% 50% #2191C0;
    border: 1px solid #4297D7; color: #EAF5F7; font-weight:
    bold; -moz-border-radius: 4px; -webkit-border-radius:
    4px; border-radius: 4px; }

#caltitle { font-size:14px; float:left; text-align:center;
    width: 155px; line-height: 20px; color: #EAF5F7; font-
    weight: bold; }

#calnext, #calprev { display:block; width: 16px; height:
    20px; float:left; cursor:pointer; margin-top: 2px; }
```

```
#calnext {
  background:transparent url(ui-icons_056b93_256x240.png)
  no-repeat scroll center center; background-position:
  -48px -192px; float:right; margin-right: 4px; }

#calprev {
  background:transparent url(ui-icons_056b93_256x240.png)
  no-repeat scroll center center; background-position:
  -78px -192px; margin-left: 4px; }

#caldays { margin-top: 3px; }

#caldays span { display: block; float: left; width: 30px;
                text-align: center; }

  /* single day */
  .calweek a { background: url("ui-bg_gloss-
  wave_75_2191c0_500x100.png") repeat-x scroll 50% 50% #0078AE;
  border: 1px solid #77D5F7; -moz-border-radius: 3px;
  -webkit-border-radius: 3px; border-radius: 3px;
  color: #FFFFFF; display: block; float: left; font-size: 11px;
  font-weight: normal; height: 18px; line-height: 20px;
  margin-left: 2px; outline: medium none; text-align:
  center; text-decoration: none; width: 26px; }

  /* current day */
  #calcurrent, #caltoday {
    background: url("ui-bg_gloss-wave_50_6eac2c_500x100.png")
    repeat-x scroll 50% 50% #6EAC2C; border: 1px solid #ACDD4A;
    color: #FFF; font-weight: normal; outline: medium none;
    z-index:9999; }

  /* today */
  #caltoday {
    background: url("images/ui-bg_gloss-
    wave_45_e14f1c_500x100.png") repeat-x scroll 50% 50% #6EAC2C;
    border: 1px solid #ACDD4A; color: #000;
  }
```

If all is well, you will have a calendar that is similar in appearance to that of jQuery UI's version, but perhaps without the same amount of code! Here's a screenshot of what you should see:

A final thought

The code above is not perfect—it was designed as a concept of what could be possible when using elements from jQuery UI's themes in DateInput. The jQuery UI has a number of themes available, from which elements could easily be used to provide similar effects within your code. It is key to understand that I am not using jQuery UI's Javascript, as this will add a large amount of additional code to your site, which is against the whole ethos of jQuery Tools. That all said, there is nothing stopping you from using elements from the themes!

There is a barebones version of the `skin` file available to download from the main jQuery Tools site—in some respects, you may find it more desirable to work from this, rather than try to adjust an existing theme. However, a lot of this will depend on the changes you want to make—if you are not making many, then it might be more sensible to simply override the existing `skin` file, rather than create additional work for yourself.

Controlling your HTML5 range input with RangeInput

The advent of HTML5 is bringing with it a number of additional types that can be used with the `<input>` command, such as `<input type="range">`. Whilst this may be good news for developers, it is not so good for those who still have to work with older browsers, as this effect will only work natively in the most recent browsers.

Enter jQuery Tools' RangeInput, which makes the same effect available to all browsers (with the exception of IE5 and IE6, as the market share for these browsers is now so small that the lack of support for these two browsers will not affect the majority of your website audiences).

Why basic RangeInput?

The jQuery Tools is designed to standardize the HTML5 functionality of `<input type="range">` across all modern browsers, ready for when it is officially released, and the majority of browsers support it by default. As jQuery Tools abstracts a lot of the styling and inherent power away into its CSS, it will just be a matter of removing this, to allow the HTML5 functionality to work.

Let's dive into this a little more, to see how it would work in a normal environment.

Usage

All of the Tools follow the same basic principle of requiring minimal JavaScript to operate, with CSS styling providing the real power—RangeInput is no exception. The basic format falls into three parts – the first is the link to the CSS that provides the styling required by RangeInput, the second is at least one `<input>` statement (the following code shows two—the same principle applies for both), followed by the call to RangeInput from the Tools library:

```
<!-- styling for the range -->
<link rel="stylesheet" type="text/css" href="range.css"/>

<!-- a couple of HTML5 range inputs with standard attributes -->
<input type="range" name="range1" min="50" max="500" step="20"
value="100" />
<input type="range" name="range2" min="0" max="1500" step="50"
value="450" />

<!-- select all range inputs and make them ranges -->
<script>
  $(":range").rangeinput();
</script>
```

Now, most of the people might think that a RangeInput should really be used to obtain a value from a preset scale, displayed on a website. This is a perfectly valid assumption, but only a small part of what RangeInput could be used to do. To prove this, let's have a look at the project to build a scrollable product gallery—this one will display a number of books, and could easily be used on a retail website, such as Packt's.

Project: building a product gallery

We're going to build a basic scrollable product gallery, in a style used by the PC manufacturer Apple™ some years ago. The inspiration for this project came from a tutorial available online, from `http://jqueryfordesigners.com/slider-gallery/`, that explains how to create a similar effect using jQuery—which is a perfect excuse to show off how versatile jQuery Tools' RangeInput really is, and how it can be used to produce the same effect!

Although the basic framework will remain the same, this is something for which you could easily alter the styles at a later date, as you see fit. Let's begin with setting up the basic structure.

Setting up the basic HTML structure

Open up the text editor of your choice, and insert the following lines Then save this as your HTML page:

```
<!DOCTYPE html>
<html>
  <head>
    <title>jQuery Tools standalone demo</title>

    <!-- include the Tools -->
    <script src="http://ajax.googleapis.com/
    ajax/libs/jquery/1.6.4/jquery.min.js">
    </script>
    <script src="https://raw.github.com/jquerytools/jquerytools/
    master/src/rangeinput/rangeinput.js"></script>
  </head>
  <body>
    <div id="wrap">
      <!-- our scrollable element -->
      <div id="scrollwrap">
      <div id="scroll">
      <ul>
      </ul>
    </div>
    </div>
    <!-- rangeinput that controls the scroll -->
    <input type="range" max="2600" step="10" />
    </div>
    <script>
    </script>
  </body>
</html>
```

Now, we have our basic framework, let's start adding the content.

You will note that in the demo, we have linked directly to the source file for Tools, that is hosted in Github. This is acceptable, but should only be for the purposes of development; if you are using this in a production environment, you will need to change to using one of the CDN links, or a downloaded copy of the library.

Adding in the book images

Next come the images of the books we need to add in; we're using 30 in all. If you want to use fewer, then this is possible, but you will need to alter the styling around the slider, to allow for the change in the number of images used.

Add the following in between the `<ul> </ul>` tags in your code:

```
<li><img src="books/4569.jpg" /><span class="textfont">Test Book 1
</span></li>
<li><img src="books/6860.jpg" /><span>Test Book 2</span></li>
<li><img src="books/4408.jpg" /><span>Test Book 3</span></li>
<li><img src="books/6785.jpg" /><span>Test Book 4</span></li>
<li><img src="books/2305.jpg" /><span>Test Book 5</span></li>
<li><img src="books/1925.jpg" /><span>Test Book 6</span></li>
<li><img src="books/1308.jpg" /><span>Test Book 7</span></li>
<li><img src="books/5108.jpg" /><span>Test Book 8</span></li>
<li><img src="books/6884.jpg" /><span>Test Book 9</span></li>
<li><img src="books/4323.jpg" /><span>Test Book 10</span></li>
<li><img src="books/4569.jpg" /><span>Test Book 11</span></li>
<li><img src="books/6860.jpg" /><span>Test Book 12</span></li>
<li><img src="books/4408.jpg" /><span>Test Book 13</span></li>
<li><img src="books/6785.jpg" /><span>Test Book 14</span></li>
<li><img src="books/2305.jpg" /><span>Test Book 15</span></li>
<li><img src="books/1925.jpg" /><span>Test Book 16</span></li>
<li><img src="books/1308.jpg" /><span>Test Book 17</span></li>
<li><img src="books/5108.jpg" /><span>Test Book 18</span></li>
<li><img src="books/6884.jpg" /><span>Test Book 19</span></li>
<li><img src="books/4323.jpg" /><span>Test Book 20</span></li>
<li><img src="books/4569.jpg" /><span>Test Book 21</span></li>
<li><img src="books/6860.jpg" /><span>Test Book 22</span></li>
<li><img src="books/4408.jpg" /><span>Test Book 23</span></li>
<li><img src="books/6785.jpg" /><span>Test Book 24</span></li>
<li><img src="books/2305.jpg" /><span>Test Book 25</span></li>
<li><img src="books/1925.jpg" /><span>Test Book 26</span></li>
<li><img src="books/1308.jpg" /><span>Test Book 27</span></li>
<li><img src="books/5108.jpg" /><span>Test Book 28</span></li>
<li><img src="books/6884.jpg" /><span>Test Book 29</span></li>
<li><img src="books/4323.jpg" /><span>Test Book 30</span></li>
```

In this example, we're using images from Packt's website — you are free to use other images if you desire, although you will need to keep to a similar size, or adjust the styling to suit.

Adding in the JavaScript functionality

Let's move onto adding the JavaScript functionality:

```
// get handle to the scrollable DIV
var scroll = $("#scroll");

  // initialize rangeinput
  $(":range").rangeinput({

    // slide the DIV along with the range using jQuery's css() method
    onSlide: function(ev, step) {
      scroll.css({left: -step + "px"});
    },

    // display progressbar
    progress: true,

    // the DIV is animated when the slider is clicked: function(e, i)
    {
      scroll.animate({left: -i + "px"}, "fast");
    },

    // disable drag handle animation when slider is clicked
    speed: 0
  });
```

The code above creates an instance of the internal "scrolling" DIV (that is #scroll), then use CSS to move it to the appropriate amount either left or right; this is animated by using jQuery's .animate() function to provide smoother movement.

Styling the gallery

At this stage, if you run the code, you will not see an awful lot working — that is because the true power of jQuery Tools actually lies in the CSS styling that is applied.

```
<style>
  // body, a:active and : focus only needed for demo; these can be
  // removed for production use
  body { padding:50px 80px; }
```

```
a:active { outline:none; }

focus { -moz-outline-style:none; }

#wrap {
  background:url("images/productbrowser.jpg") no-repeat scroll 0
  0 transparent;
}

/* outermost element for the scroller (stays still) */
#scrollwrap {
  position: relative;
  overflow: hidden;
  width: 620px;
  height: 150px;
  margin-bottom: 15px;
  -moz-box-shadow: 0 0 20px #666;
  -webkit-box-shadow: 0 0 20px #666;
  border-radius: 4px 4px 0 0;
}

/* the element that moves forward/backward */
#scroll {
  position:relative;
  width:20000em;
  overflow: hidden;
  padding: 20px 100px;
  height: 160px;
  color: #fff;
  text-shadow: 5px 1px 1px #000;
  left: -100px;
}

#scroll span {
  font-weight:bold;
  font-family: sans-serif;
  font-size: 12px;
  float: left;
  padding-right: 72px;
  width: 30px;
}

slider {
  background: transparent url("images/bkgrdhandle.png") no-repeat
  scroll 0 0 transparent;
  position: relative;
  cursor: pointer;
  height: 17px;
  width: 580px;
```

```
      -moz-border-radius: 2px;
      -webkit-border-radius: 2px;
      border-radius: 2px
      margin-top: -10px;
      padding: 3px;
      margin-left: 16px;
      background-size: 581px auto;
   }
   handle {
      -moz-border-radius: 14px;
      -webkit-border-radius: 14px;
      border-radius: 14px;
      cursor: move;
      display: block;
      height: 18px;
      position: absolute;
      top: 0;       width: 181px;
      background: url("images/scroller.png") no-repeat scroll
      0 0 transparent;
   }
   handle:active {
      background-color: #00f;
   }
   range {
      display:none;
   }
   #scroll ul {
      list-style: none outside none;
      margin: 0;
      padding: 0;
      position: absolute;
      white-space: nowrap;
      left: 40px;
   }
   #scroll ul li {
      display: inline;
      width: 80px;
   }
   #scroll ul li img {
      padding-right: 20px;
   }
</style>
```

If all is well, then you should see something similar to this, once you have added in the styling:

Some final comments

Whilst this was built for 30 book images, this could easily have been any product images—the key to it is ensuring that either the images used are of the same size, or that the CSS is adjusted to ensure an even width. The beauty of jQuery Tools is that whilst JavaScript is kept to a minimum, just about every element can be tweaked using CSS—RangeInput is no exception. It is important to note that though there are some CSS3 styles used in this demo, which you may find won't work in some of the older browsers; this is something to bear in mind when using this effect in your websites. After all, the very ethos of jQuery Tools is to push forward to using more and more CSS3

Summary

In this chapter, we looked at three of the lesser known, yet still important components of jQuery Tools, namely Validator, DateInput and RangeInput. Although these may not be so well known or used as the other components, they are still equally as powerful, particularly when you allow for the level of customisability available using CSS, and where they can also be extended using jQuery (as can the other components). We took a more theoretical peek at how you can style DateInput using elements from jQuery UI—the effect here probably needs some tweaking; it is still a useful way to show off what could be done, if elements from other jQuery UI themes were also used.

In the fourth and final chapter of this book, we will be delving into the world of Expose and FlashEmbed, which in themselves are not necessarily used on their own, but are still important parts of the jQuery Tools library.

4
jQuery Tools Toolbox

Phew! We've taken a real whistle-stop tour through the jQuery Tools library, and looked at some exciting features that you can use in your own projects.

Time for a rest, methinks…Not so fast, my friend! We still have one more section to look at, Toolbox.

Toolbox? What's this all about then?

It's a small collection of tools that can be used with the main tools from the library—think of it as using an extension arm on a socket set, for example. This Toolbox includes functionality that allows embedding of Flash movies, as well as being able to go backwards in your browser, or control your mousewheel within your pages.

Let's get started and look at each in a little more detail, beginning with FlashEmbed.

It is very likely that there will be significant changes to this section of the jQuery Tools library in future versions—as you will see, it contains functionality that is fast becoming superseded by advances in HTML5, CSS3, and jQuery. I've included it in this book to make you aware of what is still possible, although most likely, it will not be backward compatible with version 2 of jQuery Tools when that becomes available on general release.

Using FlashEmbed to include Flash movies

Adobe's Flash™ technology became the de facto standard for embedding Flash-based movies into web pages, and since its introduction in 1996, it has been developed for use on a wide variety of platforms, including Linux, Tablet PC, Blackberries, and of course, Windows.

The downside of this capability is that not every browser works with the same embedding code – enter jQuery Tools' FlashEmbed, which allows you to embed Flash using the same configuration options, while the library handles the backend embedding code.

 Note: The advances in JavaScript and HTML5 technology are beginning to make the use of Flash embedding technology redundant, as most modern CSS3-based browsers are able to handle videos using the `<video>` tag, without the need for additional software. It is very likely that FlashEmbed may disappear from future versions of this library, once HTML5 and CSS3 become more widespread and older browsers such as IE5 and IE6 disappear from use.

Usage

Embedding Flash files is simplicity itself; there are three parts to set up a basic Flash capability in your web pages.

HTML setup

First you need to include the FlashEmbed script on your page:

```
<script type="text/javascript" src="toolbox.flashembed.min.js">
</script>
```

In keeping with the principle ethos of jQuery Tools, it is recommended that you use the minified version of the library to keep the download times as low as possible. You then need to have a HTML container for the object; we are using a DIV element in our example. This has an id attribute to reference this container later in the embedding:

```
<div id="clock"></div>
```

JavaScript setup

We then use FlashEmbed to place a Flash object in the previous container, copy this into your web page:

```
flashembed("clock", "/swf/clock.swf");
```

The call must be placed after the DIV element or you must place it inside a $(document).ready() block with jQuery.

Demo: let's embed a Flash movie

Unlike other projects in this book, we are not going to try to build something useful for a potential client, but have a look at FlashEmbed, and how you could use it to embed Flash, while still maintaining support for older browsers.

With this in mind, let's set up a basic HTML structure, using the following code:

```html
<!DOCTYPE html>
<html>
<head>
    <title>jQuery Tools standalone demo</title>

    <!-- include the Tools -->
    <script src=
     "http://cdn.jquerytools.org/1.2.6/full/jquery.tools.min.js">
     </script>

    <!-- standalone page styling (can be removed) -->
    <link rel="stylesheet" type="text/css"
     href="http://static.flowplayer.org/tools/css/standalone.css"/>
</head>
<body>
</body>
</html>
```

Space for the video

We need to include a space on the page for the video, so copy in the following code to your webpage:

```html
<div id="flash2">
    <img src="play_text_large.png" alt="" />
</div>
```

Styling for the video

We need to add a little extra styling, the following code will reset the fonts used, and centre the video on the page; the styling for #flash2 will add a play button in the middle of the image:

```
<style>

#flash2 { width: 787px; height: 300px; background-
         image: url(splash.jpg); text-align:center;
         cursor:pointer; }

#flash2 img { margin-top: 110px; }
</style>
```

Script to make the video work

The FlashEmbed tool available in jQuery Tools does not require the use of jQuery to function, although it is supported if you need it; this is an example of how you could use it. Copy the following script into the <head> section:

```
<script>
// use the jQuery alternative for flashembed.domReady
$(function() {

    // bind an onClick event for this second Flash container
    $("#flash2").click(function() {

        // same as in previous example
        $(this).flashembed("http://static.flowplayer.org/swf/flash10.
swf");
    });
});
</script>
```

If everything worked fine, then you should see a video play, as follows:

Some final comments

While Flash is still very useful, it is fast becoming an old technology; early iPads and other products did not support it, although this is changing for later models. However, HTML5 and JavaScript are taking over—HTML5 includes support for the `<canvas>` and `<video>` tags, without the need for additional support. This allows for many Flash-like behaviors and visualizations to be built with simple HTML, CSS, and JavaScript; images could equally be used, although in many cases, they won't be required. Support for both tags is still mixed, with better support in WebKit and Mozilla-based browsers than in Internet Explorer; FlashEmbed comes into its own by allowing Flash to be played in older browsers, using a common standard—the library handles the different embedding code required.

On a different note, you can also use FlashEmbed to embed fonts, using the SIFR technology; this should be used with caution, as the technology hasn't been updated for quite some time. Browsers contain support for `@font-face`, which allows the display of fonts in all major browsers including IE6-9, Firefox, Chrome, and Safari, without the need for additional external libraries. SIFR will only work for embedding small Flash files, as it is processor-intensive and carries a big overhead for very little extra benefit—you should use it with care!

Moving on, let's now take a look at the history plugin, that is available as part of jQuery Tools.

Going backwards with history

A key part of navigating around the web is the ability to control the direction we travel. While this may sound a little odd, there are occasions when we need to go backwards, to revisit something we've already viewed. This doesn't always work, depending on the environment—this is where the history plugin can help.

Usage

This is a simple plugin tool that allows you to take control of the browser's history. This means that as and when you navigate back and forth through pages, the browser's buttons will be notified, so you can use them to navigate correctly.

It should be noted though that while the history function can be called using code such as the following, it is more likely that you will use this as a configuration option within one of the tools, such as Tabs or Scrollable:

```
$("a.links_with_history").history(function(event, hash) {

});
```

To illustrate how this could be used with something such as Tabs, have a look at the following code:

```
$(function() {
    $("#flowtabs").tabs("#flowpanes > div", { history: true });
});
```

This will reference the same history functionality that is available separately within the jQuery Tools library. If used correctly, you will be able to navigate backward and forward using the browser's buttons—if you navigate through each tab of a Tab, for example, then using the **Back** button will take you back through each tab that you've visited, in the order of visit:

The URLs that are generated will look similar to the following:

```
http://flowplayer.org/tools/demos/tabs/history.html#streaming_tab
```

You can bookmark these URLs in the normal manner; if you bookmark one of these links, and return to it later, you will be able to load that specific "section". In this example, it will load the specific tab that has been referenced by the requested URL.

It is important to note that although this is described as an HTML5 library, the current release of Tools (version 1.2.6, at the time of writing) is not able to handle certain formats that are otherwise standard for HTML5. For example, you can use `http://flowplayer.org/tools/demos/tabs/history.html#123`, but you won't be able to use something like: `http://flowplayer.org/tools/demos/tabs/history.html/#/page/#SecondTab`.

Let's now have a look at another component of the Toolbox, Expose.

Showing off content with Expose

If you run a website where it is necessary to highlight information or content, such as displaying a video, then you will most likely find a need to make the background less of a distraction. Such an effect is used very well by some TV companies, when they display content for playback via the Internet—it's akin to *switching the lights off*, when you want to watch a good movie.

Expose is a tool that can help here. It exposes or *highlights* a particular element, and fades out the others, so that you can only see what the website owner intended. There is a quirk though with this tool. Normally you would not use this on its own, but as part of the Overlay tool featured earlier in this book. However, Expose has been developed to take this concept further, and work as a standalone tool or one integrated into Overlay. It doesn't matter in which *mode* it is used but you can use it to expose all manner of objects, such as images, forms, or Flash objects. We're going to use it to show off a video. Before doing so, lets take a look at it in a little more detail.

Usage

jQuery Tools' Expose is very easy to configure, although its versatility means that you can use it to great effect in a number of ways:

```
// place a white mask over the page
$(document).mask();

// place a custom colored mask over the page
$(document).mask("#789");

// place a non-closable mask - this effectively makes it a modal mask
$(document).mask{ closeOnEsc: false, closeOnClick: false });
```

```
// place a mask but let selected elements show through (expose)
$("div.to_be_exposed").expose();

// close the mask
$.mask.close();
```

 The default color for `.mask` is white, this can be overridden by specifying a HTML color as shown in the preceding second example, or you can use the `color` attribute within your call to Expose/Mask.

Now, the observant among you will notice that there were calls to two different functions in the preceding code; this is because there are effectively two different ways to expose content: using `mask` and `expose`.

The `mask` function will only be available for the document object. It does not work with any other selector. This means that if you want to use it to show off elements contained in a `DIV`, for example, then you will need to use the `expose` function. All elements returned by the expose selector will be placed on top of the mask.

The `mask` function (which loads immediately after the expose or mask call) can use different configurations on each call; if a configuration is not specified, then it will automatically use the last configuration supplied in the previous call. By default, the tool is set to use any element if its ID is set to `exposeMask`, although you can alter the configuration to specify your own if you are using this ID for some other purpose.

As we will see in the demo, `mask` and `expose` both need to be closed and their configurations destroyed, before a new one can be created with new attributes that are different to the existing `mask` or `expose`.

Demo: using Expose to display video content

One of the great features of jQuery Tools is that its components can easily be combined with others in the library, or be extended with the use of additional jQuery. One such example, which we are going to look at, is the use of Expose with Overlay. This demo will take you through how you can combine the two to great effect. This borrows from a fine example, which is available from the main jQuery Tools website.

This demo will use the Overlay functionality, similar to that used in *Chapter 2, Getting along with your UI Tools*, along with the "Flowplayer" video tool, available from `http://www.flowplayer.org`.

Setting up the basic HTML structure

Lets begin by setting up the basic structure for the video content. This is very similar to the projects we looked at earlier in the book, although you will note the inclusion of "Flowplayer":

```html
<!DOCTYPE html>
<html>
<head>
    <title>jQuery Tools standalone demo</title>

    <!-- include the Tools -->
    <script src="http://cdn.jquerytools.org/1.2.6/full/jquery.tools.
min.js"></script>

    <script src="flowplayer-3.2.6.min.js"></script>

    <!-- standalone page styling (can be removed) -->
    <link rel="stylesheet" type="text/css" href="http://static.
flowplayer.org/tools/css/standalone.css"/>

    <script>
    </script>
</head>
<body>
</body>
</html>
```

 Flowplayer is written by Tero Piirainen, who is also the main developer of jQuery Tools. You can download a free version of the excellent video tool from `http://flowplayer.org/download/index.html`.

Adding the video content

Now that we have a basic structure in place, we need to start adding in some content. The following code sets up the trigger that fires off the overlay, followed by the overlay that contains the video to be displayed. Note that you can include multiple examples on the same page, while the Overlay tool can be customised to use different overlay backgrounds; the Expose tool is known as a *singleton*. This means that a single instance and configuration is shared for every usage, no matter how many times it is used.

```html
<h2>Multiple overlay demo</h2>

<p>
    <button rel="#overlay1">Video 1</button>
```

```
      <button rel="#overlay2">Video 2</button>
</p>

<!-- overlays for both videos -->
<div class="overlay" id="overlay1">
    <a class="player" href="http://pseudo01.hddn.com/vod/demo.
flowplayervod/flowplayer-700.flv">
         
    </a>
</div>

<div class="overlay" id="overlay2">
    <a class="player" href="http://pseudo01.hddn.com/vod/demo.
flowplayervod/flowplayer-700.flv">
         
    </a>
</div>
```

Adding the styling

The next stage is to add in the all-important styling—there is no great deal needed, and most of it is needed for the Overlay to function properly:

```
<style>
.overlay { background:url(white.png) no-repeat; padding:40px;
           width:576px; display:none; }

.close {
    background: url(close.png) no-repeat;
    position: absolute;
    top: 2px;
    display: block;
    right: 5px;
    width: 35px;
    height: 35px;
    cursor: pointer;
}

a.player { display:block; height: 450px; }
</style>
```

Getting the player to work

The final step involved is to add the script that makes the overlay and video work:

```
$(function() {

    // setup overlay actions to buttons
    $("button[rel]").overlay({

        // use the Apple effect for overlay
        effect: 'apple',

        expose: '#789',

        onLoad: function(content) {
        // find and load the player contained in the overlay
            this.getOverlay().find("a.player").flowplayer(0).load();
        },

        onClose: function(content) {
            $f().unload();
        }
    });

    // install flowplayers
    $("a.player").flowplayer(
"http://releases.flowplayer.org/swf/flowplayer-3.2.7.swf");
    });
```

If all is well, you should see something like this:

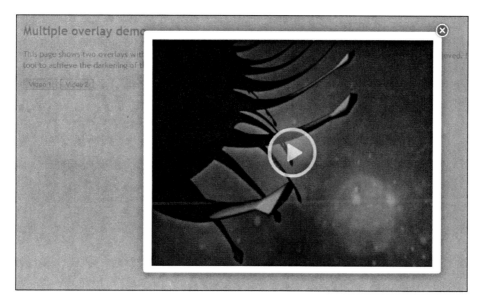

Let's now have a look at the final component in the Toolbox part of the library, which is mousewheel.

Take control of your mouse with mousewheel

The final part of the Toolbox group of components is mousewheel – this allows you to take control of the mouse wheel, when navigating around a page using a jQuery Tools tool.

Usage

The code for enabling mousewheel is very simple. It involves one call to the mousewheel library, where `event` is the jQuery event object being controlled, and `delta` is the amount of movement in the mousewheel. A positive value means that the wheel is being moved up, while a negative value means that the wheel is being moved downwards:

```
// make #myelement listen for mousewheel events
$("#myelement").mousewheel(function(event, delta) {

});
```

However, you should note that mousewheel really comes into its own when used as a configuration option in the main UI Toolset, such as Scrollable. While it exists as a separate library, it is more likely that you won't reference it using the preceding method, but as part of the configuration of another tool.

To demonstrate, lets have a look at the code for a basic scroll, which has mousewheel enabled:

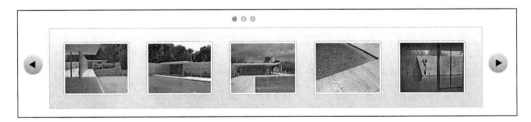

Now, from looking at the previous screenshot, you would not immediately be able to tell if it had the mousewheel functionality, correct? Yes, that is correct, it doesn't add anything to the visual appearance of the tool being used. The only way to tell is by looking at the code, which would probably look similar to the following:

```
$("#chained").scrollable({circular: true, mousewheel: true}).
navigator().autoscroll({
    interval: 3000
});
```

Although it is a configuration option here, it is actually referencing the mousewheel library, which may or may not already be included in your projects, depending on the version of jQuery Tools you have downloaded (by default, it is not included in some of the CDN links, for example, so this would either require a change of link, or an additional call to the mousewheel functionality, as a separate custom download).

Summary

In this chapter, we had a look at the third and final part of jQuery Tools, in the form of Toolbox. We've learnt how to expose objects on a page, using Expose, and that this is actually used as a basis for the main Overlay functionality from *Chapter 2, Getting along with your UI Tools*. We also looked at FlashEmbed—even though the technology is arguably being superseded by the advances of HTML5 functionality in newer browsers, it can still play a vital role in older browsers for as long as they still exist. Then we learned about mousewheel and history, and how although you may use them separately in your projects, it is more likely that you will use them as a configuration option in one of the many tools that make up the jQuery Tools library.

In the meantime, I hope you've enjoyed reading this book, as much as I have enjoyed writing it, and that you've found something useful that you can use for your future projects.

 If I've piqued your interest, and you would like to see how jQuery Tools could be used in a real environment, such as a CMS, then don't forget to download the PDF that comes with this book. It contains some good examples of using Tools within a CMS, using the popular WordPress system. Enjoy!

Index

Symbols

$(document).ready() block **81**
<a> markup **30**
<canvas> tag **83**
<head> area **61**
<head> section **82**
<iframe> markup **30**
<input> command **71**
 jQuery, toolbox **79**
[title] attribute **35**
<ul> tag **74**
<video> tag **80, 83**

A

Application Programming Interface (API)
  best practices **18, 19**
  event listeners, supplying from **21**

B

basic HTML structure
  setting up **87**
bind method
  using **20**
buttons
  adding, to slideshow **50, 51**
button visibility
  setting **52, 53**

C

callbacks 19
CDN 13
CDN links
  about **91**

  using **13**
Chrome 83
code
  adding, for overlay trigger **30**
color attribute 86
CSS3 79
CSS role, jQuery Tools 9
custom field validators
  adding **57**
custom validators 61-64

D

data validation 56
DateInput
  about **66**
  basic HTML structure, creating **67, 68**
  JavaScript, setting up **68, 69**
  localization **67**
  overview **71**
  styling **67**
  styling, adding **69, 71**
  usage **66, 67**
div element 8, 81
dl element 8
document.ready() function 61
download builder
  about **14**
  using **14**
downloading
  jQuery Tools library **12**

E

errorClass option 63
errorInputEvent option 63

position option 62
preventDefault() method 22
product gallery
  building 73
  styling 75, 78

R

RangeInput
  about 71
  basic HTML structure, setting up 73
  book images, adding 74, 75
  JavaScript, setting up 75
  need for 72
  overview 78
  product gallery, building 73
  product gallery, styling 75, 78
  usage 72
rel attribute 29
rel tag 52
reset method 65
rolling slideshow
  building 47-50

S

Safari 66, 83
Scrollable
  about 39
  basic HTML structure, setting up 40-42
  basic structure 39, 40
  JavaScript, setting up 42-44
  mini gallery, building 40
  styles 44, 45
speed option 62

T

Tab effects
  configuring 51
Tablet PC 80
Tabs
  about 46
  basic HTML structure, setting up 47, 48
  basic structure 46
  button visibility, setting 52, 53
  visual effects, adding 48

tabs functionality 9
this variable 20, 21
title attribute 34
tooltip CSS styles
  adding 36
Tooltips
  about 34
  basic HTML, setting up 36
  configuring 37, 38
  creating, for allowing purchase of books 35
  dynamic plugins 35
  setting up 34
  slide effects 35
  usage 34

U

UI tools
  about 28
  overlays 28
  Scrollable 39, 40
  Tabs 46
  Tooltips 34
ul element 8

V

Validators
  about 55
  basic HTML structure, creating 57
  form details, adding 58, 59
  form, styling 59, 61
  limitations 65
  need for 56
  overview 66
  usage 56, 57
video content
  adding 87
  displaying, Expose used 86
viewer
  building, for Google Maps 29

W

Web 2.0 8

Thank you for buying
jQuery Tools UI Library

About Packt Publishing

Packt, pronounced 'packed', published its first book "*Mastering phpMyAdmin for Effective MySQL Management*" in April 2004 and subsequently continued to specialize in publishing highly focused books on specific technologies and solutions.

Our books and publications share the experiences of your fellow IT professionals in adapting and customizing today's systems, applications, and frameworks. Our solution based books give you the knowledge and power to customize the software and technologies you're using to get the job done. Packt books are more specific and less general than the IT books you have seen in the past. Our unique business model allows us to bring you more focused information, giving you more of what you need to know, and less of what you don't.

Packt is a modern, yet unique publishing company, which focuses on producing quality, cutting-edge books for communities of developers, administrators, and newbies alike. For more information, please visit our website: www.packtpub.com.

About Packt Open Source

In 2010, Packt launched two new brands, Packt Open Source and Packt Enterprise, in order to continue its focus on specialization. This book is part of the Packt Open Source brand, home to books published on software built around Open Source licences, and offering information to anybody from advanced developers to budding web designers. The Open Source brand also runs Packt's Open Source Royalty Scheme, by which Packt gives a royalty to each Open Source project about whose software a book is sold.

Writing for Packt

We welcome all inquiries from people who are interested in authoring. Book proposals should be sent to author@packtpub.com. If your book idea is still at an early stage and you would like to discuss it first before writing a formal book proposal, contact us; one of our commissioning editors will get in touch with you.

We're not just looking for published authors; if you have strong technical skills but no writing experience, our experienced editors can help you develop a writing career, or simply get some additional reward for your expertise.

jQuery UI Themes Beginner's Guide

ISBN: 978-1-84951-044-8   Paperback: 268 pages

Create new themes for your jQuery site with this step-by-step guide

1. Learn the details of the jQuery UI theme framework by example

2. No prior knowledge of jQuery UI or theming frameworks is necessary

3. The CSS structure is explained in an easy-to-understand and approachable way

4. Numerous examples, no unnecessary long explanations, lots of screenshots and diagrams

jQuery 1.4 Animation Techniques: Beginners Guide

ISBN: 978-1-849513- 30-2   Paperback: 344 pages

Quickly master all of jQuery's animation methods and build a toolkit of ready-to-use animations using jQuery 1.4

1. Create both simple and complex animations using clear, step-by-step instructions, accompanied with screenshots

2. Walk through each of jQuery's built-in animation methods and see in detail how each one can be used

3. Over 50 detailed examples of different types of web page animations

Please check **www.PacktPub.com** for information on our titles

Learning jQuery, Third Edition

ISBN: 978-1-84951-654-9   Paperback: 428 pages

Create better interaction, design, and web development with simple JavaScript techniques

1. An introduction to jQuery that requires minimal programming experience

2. Detailed solutions to specific client-side problems

3. Revised and updated version of this popular jQuery book

jQuery UI 1.7: The User Interface Library for jQuery

ISBN: 978-1-847199-72-0   Paperback: 392 pages

Build highly interactive web applications with ready-to-use widgets from the jQuery User Interface library

1. Organize your interfaces with reusable widgets: accordions, date pickers, dialogs, sliders, tabs, and more

2. Enhance the interactivity of your pages by making elements drag-and-droppable, sortable, selectable, and resizable

3. Packed with examples and clear explanations of how to easily design elegant and powerful front-end interfaces for your web applications

Please check **www.PacktPub.com** for information on our titles

CPSIA information can be obtained at www.ICGtesting.com
Printed in the USA
LVOW131934240212

270316LV00003B/21/P